W9-BIB-774

BLACK

THE HISTORY OF AFRICAN AMERICANS IN BASKETBALL

HOOPS

FREDRICK McKISSACK, JR.

SCHOLASTIC PRESS • NEW YORK

Copyright © 1999 by Fredrick McKissack, Jr.

Library of Congress Cataloging-in-Publication Data

McKissack, Fredrick
Black hoops: The history of African Americans in basketball / by Fredrick
L. McKissack, Jr.—1st ed.   p.   cm.
Summary: Surveys the history of African Americans in basketball from the
beginning of the sport to the present, discussing individual teams and players
and the integration of the National Basketball Association.

ISBN 0-590-48712-4 (hardcover)

1. Basketball—United States—History—Juvenile literature.
2. Afro-American basketball players—History—Juvenile literature.
[1. Afro-American basketball players—History.   2. Basketball—
History.]
I. Title   II. Title: African-Americans in basketball.
GV883.M316   1999
796.323'089'96073—dc21
98-14107   CIP   AC

10 9 8 7 6 5 4 3 2 1   9/9 0/0 01 02 03

Printed in the U.S.A. 37
First Edition, February 1999
Design by David Caplan
Photo Research by Zoe Moffitt

To Pat and Fred McKissack
for their love and support
and typing skills.

To Lisa M. Beringer,
for "Ella-ing" and trips
to Eureka Joe's in Madison.

Contents

Chapter 1

Basketball's Genesis

When you ask people about basketball, they might talk about high-flying slam dunks, crashing bodies diving for loose balls, last second three-point shot heroics, the heavy-sounding thud of a center rejecting a weak shot, and peach baskets. *Peach baskets?* Well, that's where the story of the game begins, in the late fall of 1891.

The students at the International Training School of the Young Men's Christian Association (YMCA) in Springfield, Massachusetts, were taught to have respect for education and religion. But according to the school's director of physical education, Dr. Luther Gulick, "bodily vigor . . . enables us to live on higher levels, to keep up to the top of our achievement." This link between religion and athletics became known as "muscular Christianity."

The problem Gulick faced was what to do with his students during the winter months, when it was too cold to play football and baseball. Apparently the stu-

Dr. Luther Gulick's request for a sport that would keep his students busy during the winter months resulted in the invention of basketball. [Kautz Family YMCA Archives, University of Minnesota Libraries]

dents were bored with the daily routine of calisthenics, gymnastics, and marching. Their boredom led them to undisciplined and disruptive behavior.

Gulick needed an indoor winter sport for two reasons: to keep his students busy and to keep their behavior in line with the ideals of the school. He turned to two subordinates to come up with a new game, both of whom failed. He then gave the assignment to Dr. James Naismith, a thirty-year-old Canadian teacher.

Naismith, a man known for his thick beard and intense

nature, played soccer, rugby, and lacrosse and had been on the tumbling and track teams at McGill University in Montreal. He was selected McGill's best athlete twice and later played professional lacrosse for the Montreal Shamrocks. For all his accomplishments, it should be noted that Naismith, at least by today's standards, was not a large man: 5 feet 10 inches tall and 160 pounds.

After graduating in 1887, he taught physical education at McGill and studied theology at Presbyterian College in Montreal. He received his theology degree in 1890, but Naismith didn't go the ordination route that his fellow students took. Instead he turned to the Young Men's Christian Association as a way of developing his two great passions into a profession: sports and the ministry.

Naismith moved to Springfield, Massachusetts, during the 1890–91 school year with the intent of completing the YMCA's physical education director's course. He was a center on the International Training School's football team and played with another sports legend, Amos Alonzo Stagg, who would become one the greatest football coaches of all time. In fact, Naismith made his mark in football by creating the first helmet, a set of muffs that went over the center's ears.

Naismith might not have been given the daunting task of inventing a new sport had it not been for comments he made about this particular group of 18 young men that had become hard to handle.

Dr. James Naismith, the "Father of Basketball." [UPI/Corbis-Bettmann]

"The trouble is not with the men but with the system we are using," he would say at faculty meetings. "The kind of work for this particular class should be of a recreative nature, something that would appeal to their play instincts."

Naismith tried simple games at first, which didn't hold the group's attention, and then variations of football and rugby, which were either not tough enough or too rough. Naismith soon became discouraged, but just as it seemed hopeless, he struck upon an idea that came from his childhood in Canada: Duck on the Rock.

"He remembered the most effective way of knocking off the duck [a rock] was to throw one's own rock in an arc so that it would not go far if it missed the guard's rock," writes James W. Patterson in *Cages to Jump Shots*.

Naismith reasoned that if the goals were horizontal, set on posts, scoring would require skill and finesse rather than brute strength.

The next morning Naismith asked the school janitor for two boxes. The janitor, however, only had two peach baskets—hence the name *basket*ball. Naismith mounted the baskets on the lower rail of the balcony of the gym, which happened to be 10 feet high—a standard that is still with us today.

The game was to be played with a soccer ball, and Naismith tacked rules up on the gym's bulletin board for his students to read. The 13 original rules were:

1. The ball may be thrown in any direction with one or both hands.
2. The ball may be batted in any direction with one or both hands (but never with a fist).
3. A player cannot run with the ball. The player must throw it from the spot on which he catches it, allowances to be made for a man who catches the ball when running at a good speed, if he tries to stop.
4. The ball must be held in or between the hands, the arms or the body must not be used for holding it.
5. No shouldering, holding, pushing, tripping, or striking in any way the person of an opponent shall be allowed; the first infringement of this rule by any person shall count as a foul; the second shall disqualify him until the next goal is made or, if there is evident intent to injure the person, for the whole game. No substitute allowed.
6. A foul is striking at the ball with the fist, violation of Rules 3, 4, and such as described in Rule 5.
7. If either side makes three consecutive fouls, it shall count as a goal for the opponents.
8. A goal shall be made when the ball is thrown or batted from the grounds into the basket and stays there, providing those defending the goal do not

touch or disturb the goal. If the ball rests on the edges and the opponent moves the basket, it shall count as a goal.

9. When the ball goes out of bounds, it shall be thrown into the field of play by the person first touching it. In case of a dispute, the umpire shall throw it straight onto the field. The thrower-in is allowed five seconds; if he holds it longer, it shall go to the opponent. If any side persists in delaying the game, the umpire shall call a foul on that side.

10. The umpire shall be the judge of the men and shall note the fouls and notify the referee when three consecutive fouls have been made. He shall have the power to disqualify men according to Rule 5.

11. The referee shall be the judge of the ball and shall decide when the ball is in play, in bounds, to which side it belongs, and shall keep time. He shall decide when a goal has been made, and keep account of the goals.

12. The time shall be two fifteen-minute halves, with five minutes' rest between.

13. The side making the most goals in that time shall be declared winner. In case of a draw, the game may, by agreement of the captains, be continued until another goal is made.

When the class came in later that morning, they were told by Naismith that this was his last effort in creating a new game. He divided the class into two teams of nine, selected the centers, and threw the first jump ball. There wasn't a lot written about the first game; even the score is in dispute. Some historians say several scores were made; others have the final score 1–0. What *is* known is that there were an incredible number of fouls. At times half the members of each team were in the penalty area.

The game was a hit, and within a few weeks as many as 200 people would show up to see noon-hour games.

That winter, when the students went home for Christmas break, they took the game along with them. The sport still didn't have a name, although one student suggested Naismith Ball, at which the inventor balked.

The school's newspaper, *The Triangle*, printed an article on January 15, 1892, titled "Basket Ball." The article, written by Naismith, went on to suggest that the game could be played by up to 40 people. He originally thought that nine players would be best, but felt that the more players on the court, the more fun.

His original idea for an alignment looked like a lacrosse lineup: three defenders (one goalkeeper, two guards), three centers; three offensive men (two wingers and a "home man," who would do most of the scoring).

The free throw after a penalty is a standard in today's

game, but Naismith had ruled it out for the very reasons it is so effective now. "After he had a little practice, a good thrower could convert it into a goal almost every time," Naismith wrote. He also suggested that the referees and physical education directors make sure the teams didn't get rowdy during the game.

The sport quickly caught on at YMCA branches in New England, New York, the South, and eventually California, with students launching everything from soccer balls to coconuts toward baskets nailed into trees.

"Basketball is about the youngest of the athletic games, but it has gained great popularity," announced *The New York Times* in 1894. "The game has been played with more enthusiasm than any other sport in the gymnasiums of the different associations in this country during the past Winter."

Variations on rules came about fairly rapidly during the first few years of the game. In 1893, the YMCA suggested that five-man teams be the limit for small gymnasiums; nine-man teams in larger ones. It wasn't until 1897 that the current rule of five men per team on the court was made.

In 1893, the peach basket was discarded for a 15-inch cylindrical wire basket. After each score, the referee would use a long pole to punch the ball out of the basket. In 1894, Narragansett Machine Company, of

Dr. James Naismith (center right) with the first basketball team. [Kautz Family YMCA Archives, University of Minnesota Libraries]

Providence, Rhode Island, created a wire basketball hoop, with a long cord attached. After each basket the referee would pull the cord, which would raise the wire net and force the ball out of the top. It wasn't until 1912 that the open-bottom basket was invented.

Also, during the 1894–95 season the first basketball was put into play. It was a rubber bladder encased in leather, four inches larger in diameter than a soccer ball. It was slightly larger than today's basketball.

The backboard was invented the next season, not to aid shooters but to make sure fans didn't interfere with the ball. A 4-by-6-foot screen, made of either wood or wire, was set behind each basket.

The game was slower in those days, primarily because there was a jump ball after every basket. Baskets were worth three points during basketball's early evolution, then given a value of two points during the 1895–96 season. It was also during the early 1890s that the free throw was brought into the game. The line had been 20 feet from the basket, but was moved to the current standard of 15 feet during the 1894–95 season. The two-hand dribble was outlawed in 1898.

As with baseball and football, the popularity of basketball inevitably led to the formation of professional teams. Players of the Trenton (N.J.) Basketball Team were paid to play during the 1896–97 season. The team had been part of a YMCA, and it is unclear if they left

The first basketball game was played with peach baskets—hence the name basket*ball. [UPI/Corbis-Bettmann]*

the organization or were forced out because they were playing for money.

They played at the Masonic Temple, a huge three-story building in downtown Trenton. An advertisement in a local paper, *The Daily True American*, announced that the Trenton club was going to play the Brooklyn YMCA on Saturday, November 7, 1896. The team converted the third floor social hall of the Masonic Hall into a basketball court and charged 25 cents a seat. Spectators could stand and watch for 15 cents.

The court was sealed by a cage to keep the spectators from interfering with the game. It is the first time a cage—a 12-foot-high mesh fence—was used to sur-round the court, and it was not particularly liked by basketball puritans. It did, however, make the game go faster (there wasn't an out-of-bounds area), which made the spectators go crazy.

Trenton went on to bomb Brooklyn 16–1 in front of 700 spectators. The teams played with seven players apiece, with Trenton's captain, Fred Cooper, a native of England, leading all scorers with six points. Brooklyn scored its only point on a free throw with three minutes left in the game.

The teams went out to a local restaurant to eat after the game, as the Trenton players allegedly earned $15 each for their efforts—pretty good money in those days for 40 minutes of work.

Among Trenton's future victims were several YMCAs, a

high school team, Temple University, and the University of Pennsylvania.

Basketball's importance nationwide, as well as worldwide, was solidified when the Amateur Athletic Union (AAU) began sponsoring competitions in 1897. This led to the game being introduced as an Olympic sport at the 1904 Games in St. Louis.

While the Olympics are known as an international competition, the 1904 Olympic basketball tournament featured clubs from around the United States: the Buffalo Germans, the West Side YMCA of Chicago, the Central YMCA of Chicago, the Central YMCA of St. Louis, the Missouri Athletic Club, Turner's Tigers of San Francisco, and the Xavier Athletic Club of New York.

Each team played five games in two days, with the Buffalo Germans defeating the Central YMCA of Chicago (who were the national YMCA champions) 39–28 to win the gold medal. The Germans were an outstanding team of professional players, who went on to a record of 69–19 the next season while barnstorming through the United States.

Naismith's new game also became popular at colleges around the country. The first game on the East Coast supposedly took place between two Pennsylvania schools, Haverford and Temple, in March 1895. Haverford, playing at home, defeated Temple 6–4. The same year, two teams from the Midwest played: Minneapolis State

School of Agriculture blasted Hamline of St. Paul 9–3. Two years later, Yale crushed Penn State at New Haven 32–1.

The scores didn't indicate the inferiority of the players as much as the brutality of the game. The strategy still looked a great deal like football, with players bumping and hip-checking one another, and basically doing whatever it took to keep players from scoring. The game was so brutal in its infancy that when the University of Kentucky played fellow Kentuckians' Transylvania University in 1907, the Transylvania players wore shoulder pads. The next year Charles Eliot, president of Harvard, proclaimed that basketball was more violent than football. Both sports were almost banned due to serious injuries and an occasional death. The bans, however, were narrowly averted.

Chapter 2

From the Diamond to the Court

Basketball was born as America was struggling with the issue of civil rights, as it was still recovering from the ravages of the Civil War.

The United States was less than a century and a quarter old when Naismith invented basketball. And it had been 27 years since black people in the South were freed from the bonds of slavery. Despite the Fourteenth Amendment to the United States Constitution, which made black men and women citizens after the Civil War, somehow Americans found a way to divide themselves. In 1870, Tennessee began the South's path to segregation by enacting the first law against intermarriage. It wasn't needed before, because the whole concept of black-white marriage in the South prior to the Civil War was too bizarre to consider. But if the Constitution made all men and women citizens, then it could be possible for biracial marriages and families to happen. The rest of the South followed Tennessee's lead. By 1875, Tennessee had enacted the first of the

Jim Crow laws, which banned blacks and whites from sitting in the same train cars, in depots, or on wharves.

According to the historian John Hope Franklin, most Southern states had adopted far-reaching Jim Crow laws by 1885, which included the separation of the races in schools, barber shops, restaurants, hotels, and theaters.

In 1896, the Supreme Court handed down the infamous decision in the *Plessy v. Ferguson* case. Homer Plessy, a black man, had filed a lawsuit against a Louisiana railroad because he had been forced to ride in a segregated car. The Supreme Court ruled 8 to 1 against Plessy and upheld the doctrine of "separate but equal" as the law of the land. This was the final act that would segregate the country until the 1950s. It was a ruling that would allow racism and segregation to flourish with impunity.

In most parts of the country, African Americans were denied even the most basic human rights. Racist organizations grew unchecked and committed horrible crimes without fear of retribution. Those blacks living in the South took the brunt of the attacks. It was, for example, against the law for blacks and whites to go to school together, use the same public facilities, marry, or serve on juries together. Blacks were unable to vote in some cases and, in places where it was legal, were either discouraged from voting or forced to vote for the "right" candidate. Blacks couldn't hold public office, thus making sure that no dissenting voice against these racist laws could be heard from those it affected most.

For the few who tried to buck the system outright, there was intimidation through threats, beatings, the burning of homes and businesses, and murder. For the most part, white supremacy was accepted as fact and people of other races were considered subhuman.

By the turn of the century, separation was the law.

Although sports should have and could have been the great equalizer between races, they remained as separated as the rest of America. No matter how great an athlete was, he was only seen as a great "Negro" athlete, rather than simply an American athlete.

Professional baseball, which could have had a positive effect on black-white attitudes, was no exception. Indeed, the players, managers, and owners embraced the Jim Crow laws of separate but equal in all things. The anti-black sentiments of those associated with professional baseball were never *formally* agreed to; it was an unwritten agreement.

Jackie Robinson is credited with breaking the color barrier in major league baseball in 1947, but Moses Fleetwood Walker, a catcher who played for the integrated team at Oberlin College in Ohio, was the first professional black baseball player. In 1884, he was signed by the Toledo Baseball Club in the American Association, which would later become the American League. His brother Weldy and a few others played

Jackie Robinson was famous for stealing home base. [UPI/Corbis-Bettmann]

sporadically with pro teams in the East, but the pressure to keep the game white forced these men to abandon their dreams before the end of the 1880s.

This is not to say that blacks didn't play baseball until Jackie Robinson signed with the Brooklyn Dodgers. Indeed, they did what can be described as "American": they created their own teams and leagues. Beginning in 1885 with the Cuban Giants, a club made up of the black staff at a Long Island summer inn, blacks barnstormed through the years, playing all comers and winning many times against white ball clubs. This went on until 1920, when Rube Foster, one of the best pitchers of any race in the early part of the century and one of the richest black men in the country, started the Negro National League, which featured teams such as the Kansas City Monarchs, the Chicago American Giants, and the St. Louis Giants.

The Eastern Colored League, which featured such greats as Oscar Charleston and Pop Lloyd, was formed in opposition to the Negro National League.

Once again blacks and whites came together to play the national pastime. It was another chance for people to reconsider their feelings. In 1923, the Chicago American Giants, for example, played the Detroit Tigers (minus Ty Cobb, a notorious racist) to a one-win, one-loss, one-tie series. The Detroit Stars defeated the St. Louis Browns in all three games of a series also held that autumn. And just as it had happened in the past, someone stepped in to squash any attempt to bring about a change in racial attitudes in sports. Major League Baseball Commissioner Kenesaw Mountain Landis, a Carolinian, decreed that no major-league club would be allowed to play a black baseball club in a series. Blacks and whites, however, could play each other in all-star games after the season, which were financial windfalls for all players due to the heavy attendance. They could also play with and against each other in places like Cuba and Mexico during the winter. Blacks could dress in the same locker room, sleep in the same hotel, and eat in the same restaurants in these other countries, but were separated totally in their homeland.

Black jockeys, who dominated the sport of horse racing in the nineteenth century, were also being shoved out of their sport. The same was happening in boxing.

While all blacks faced a common struggle in terms of race in America, those who first played basketball were different from those who played baseball. "In 1891, when African Americans faced limits on their rights in the voting booth, schools, and athletics, and their post-slavery culture was developing new expressions away from European-American eyes, it's not surprising that the newly minted sport of basketball would have very little impact on them for most of the decade after its invention," wrote Nelson George in *Elevating the Game.*

According to George, the first black basketball players—unlike their counterparts in baseball or boxing—were men who attended college. The young men were part of the "talented tenth," that percentage of black Americans considered to be the best and the brightest of their race, which is in stark contrast to how people portray athletes today. These early black student-athletes, George wrote, "were the sons of Northern freedmen whose love of the sport was deep but whose use of and relationship to it fit neither the 'noble primitive' stereotypes of the early 1900s or the 'greedy jock' caricatures of the 1990s."

Bryant Gumble, the founding editor of *Black Sport* magazine, has written that these young men came from relatively well-to-do families who saw sports as a sidelight to academics: "The wise student knew better than to waste his rare opportunity of obtaining a college education," Gumble wrote. "Above all, the black man was in college to study, not perform on the athletic field."

Sports scholars believe that during the first decade of the twentieth century, blacks played on white college teams around the country and in Canada. The names of the players and their statistics are hard to find because few records, for black or white athletes, were kept as consistently as they are today. For example, between 1904 and 1908 Samuel Ransom distinguished himself as a student and basketball player at Beloit College, a small liberal arts college in southern Wisconsin. Little else is known about Ransom, however. We can only imagine what his experiences might have been, playing at a school where he may have been the only black student. He will be remembered as a trailblazer in basketball.

The New England League, made up of several colleges in Massachusetts and New Hampshire, had at least one black basketball player, but the pressure on management to remove him was overwhelming. The *Indianapolis Freeman*, a black newspaper, reported on December 24, 1904, that a basketball team in Massachusetts "was fined $100 by the President of the New England League" for "moving against the color line." In many cases white college coaches flatly refused to play against a team with black players. Organizers also learned quickly that without the fans' support they couldn't make a team financially worthwhile. So they stopped trying.

With the exception of a few who played on white teams that would still accept them, most black athletes chose to play for all-black state or private colleges. Why go where you weren't wanted and suffer the indignities that would be forced upon you?

Black youths who couldn't afford college but wanted to play basketball formed their own local clubs or played on YMCA and church-sponsored teams.

One of the early black pioneers in basketball was Edwin B. Henderson, a graduate of Harvard University, where he learned the game. He didn't *play* basketball, but brought the game back with him to his hometown of Washington, D.C., in 1905.

In 1906, as the physical training instructor of the city's public schools, Henderson joined together with five other black high school and college educators to form the Interscholastic Athlete Association of the Middle States (ISAA). Two years later, schools in Washington, D.C.; Indianapolis, Indiana; Baltimore, Maryland; and Wilmington, Delaware, were competing against each other in sports, including basketball.

"In two years over forty basketball teams, averaging eight players to a team, have trained and competed under the auspices of the ISAA," Henderson wrote in

By 1906 basketball had become very popular at the black YMCAs. [Kautz Family YMCA Archives, University of Minnesota Libraries]

the association's handbook. "It is conservative to state that over 1,000 boys have played basketball in this city since the sport was introduced."

At the beginning of the century, blacks began forming basketball club teams in the bigger cities on the East Coast.

"In 1906 basketball had invaded the black YMCAs and later the YWCAs," Ocania Chalk wrote in *Pioneers of Black Sport*. "These were teams in . . . New York, Washington, Jersey City, and Philadelphia. The Smart Set Athletic Club of Brooklyn was the first organized black basketball team in 1906. Later two other teams were formed, St. Christopher's and the Marathone Athletic Club. With three clubs now formed, a league was organized and named the Olympian Athletic Club."

The Smart Set won the first Olympian Athletic League championship during the 1907–8 season. Three more teams joined the league during the 1908–9 season: Alpha Physical Culture Club, St. Cyrian Athletic Club, and the Jersey City YMCA. Despite the presence of the new teams, the Smart Set won the league championship that season.

The basketball crowds—as with baseball, track, and football within their own seasons—became a staple of black social life on Friday and Saturday winter nights. The teams would play in front of several hundred people, and then they would sponsor a dance afterward.

Edwin Henderson's work as the athletic director for

the public school system in Washington, D.C., and the growth of the Olympian Athletic League led to a challenge match between the Smart Set and the Crescent Five, 1909 champions of Henderson's Washington Interscholastic Athletic Association. This was a bad move by the kids from Crescent High School; they were brutalized by the Smart Set 27–11. To show just how much more advanced they were than the D.C. high school players, the Smart Set annihilated Armstrong High School, 18–4.

Despite the outcome for the Washington-based teams, the games were the beginning of interregional competition between clubs and schools. They began to form teams as far west as St. Louis. And although Philadelphia's schools, as well their teams, were integrated, the city's clubs were not. The Wissahickon School Club and the Stentonworth Athletic Club were the first black teams in Philadelphia.

South of Washington, D.C., and St. Louis, Missouri, was a different matter. Southerners didn't immediately pick up on basketball before 1910, primarily because there wasn't a need to, according to the late Arthur Ashe, in *Hard Road to Glory*. "Warm weather the year round lessened the impetus for a winter game," Ashe wrote. "There were no gymnasiums, equipment was poor, coaching was out of an A. G. Spaulding manual. The YMCAs had too few indoor facilities. Yet the YMCA's outdoor play offered the only hope for a time."

But even with limited resources, the YMCAs in the South played a big role in keeping black Southerners involved in basketball. "School attendance was not required for blacks in the South, and only a small minority of those between 15 and 20 years of age attended," Ashe wrote. "Consequently, if the YMCA did not have a team, there would have been no play at all."

Washington's pride may have been damaged by the bitter defeats of two of its top clubs to the Smart Set during the 1908–9 season, but their revenge would come one year later. The Twelfth Street YMCA con-

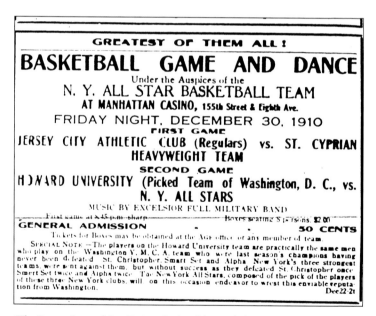

GREATEST OF THEM ALL !
BASKETBALL GAME AND DANCE
Under the Auspices of the
N. Y. ALL STAR BASKETBALL TEAM
AT MANHATTAN CASINO, 155th Street & Eighth Ave.
FRIDAY NIGHT, DECEMBER 30, 1910
FIRST GAME
JERSEY CITY ATHLETIC CLUB (Regulars) vs. ST. CYPRIAN HEAVYWEIGHT TEAM
SECOND GAME
HOWARD UNIVERSITY (Picked Team of Washington, D. C., vs. N. Y. ALL STARS
MUSIC BY EXCELSIOR FULL MILITARY BAND

First game at 8:45 p.m. sharp — Boxes seating 8 persons. $2.00

GENERAL ADMISSION - - 50 CENTS

Tickets for Boxes may be obtained at the AGE office or any member of team.

SPECIAL NOTE — The players on the Howard University team are practically the same men who play on the Washington Y. M. C. A. team, who were last season's champions having never been defeated. St. Christopher, Smart Set and Alpha, New York's three strongest teams, were sent against them, but without success as they defeated St. Christopher once, Smart Set twice and Alpha twice. The New York All Stars, composed of the pick of the players of these three New York clubs, will, on this occasion, endeavor to wrest this enviable reputation from Washington.

Dec 22-2t

The Smart Set and St. Christopher's Athletic Clubs were the first organized black basketball teams. This ad appeared in New York Age, *a popular Black magazine of the time.* [Schomburg Center for Research in Black Culture, New York Public Library; New York Age]

sisted of former high school players from the city of Washington, and became one of the better teams in the area. Twelfth Street won all 11 of its games during the 1909–10 season. They destroyed St. Christopher's of New York, 44–15, beat the Alpha Physical Culture Club three times, and defeated the Smart Set twice, once in front of more than 2,000 spectators in Brooklyn.

Women were not left out of the game during the early years. Both the Alpha Physical Culture Club and the Smart Set Athletic Club fielded women's teams. The women of the Smart Set were imitated not just for their style of play, but also for their uniforms: knee-length bloomers and long-sleeved shirts. Shorts were a big no-no at that time.

At that time, the women's game was far different from the men's. The reasons for this are vague, but were partially due to theories about women's inability to grasp the techniques of sports. Therefore, women had six players per side, rather than five, and each player had a limited number of bounces before she was forced to pass or shoot.

The two best-known women's teams after World War I were the Chicago Romas and the *Philadelphia Tribune*'s women's team. The *Tribune* was a well-known black-owned newspaper. At that time, newspapers sponsored teams in baseball, basketball, and football as a way to advertise.

The women of the *Philadelphia Tribune*'s club didn't need the paper to boost their talents. The team was made up of some of the best women basketball players on the East Coast, and they did a little barnstorming—playing from town to town, challenging all comers for money.

Chapter 3

Big-City Ball

Almost from the start the main action for blacks in basketball was on the all-black-college court. While the YMCA teams had a good following, college basketball was the key to the future development of basketball. If the "talented tenth" were playing the game and, as Edwin Henderson was, bringing the game to cities like St. Louis, Chicago, Philadelphia, Pittsburgh, and Detroit, then basketball had a chance to grow.

At that time the most popular sport in urban areas was baseball, followed by football. Basketball needed to be promoted to the black middle class in order for it to gain acceptance.

But between 1900 and 1910, the athletic programs at many black institutions were nonexistent or in an infant stage of development. While schools down South rarely had indoor gymnasiums, because the climate was warm throughout the year, cost was a factor as well. Northern colleges, even the best schools, could hardly afford gyms. Those schools that could, had gyms that can be described as dungeon-like: low ceilings, bad lighting, cramped spaces, damp, and drafty.

In February 1884, students at Washington, D.C.'s Howard University, one of the oldest black colleges in the United States, requested that a gymnasium be built. The converted gym, on one floor in an existing building, was not designed with basketball in mind, since it would be seven years before Naismith invented the game. But the gym's existence does support the claim that Howard University was one of the first black schools to have basketball as an intramural sport.

Once basketball caught on, it quickly grew in popularity. Howard's first varsity basketball team took the court in the 1910–11 season. They played their games in Spaulding Hall, a tight space actually unsuitable for basketball; but the fast-moving games were enough to generate interest and create fans.

According to writer-historian Ocania Chalk, eligibility standards were not too rigid. "Students in professional schools were allowed to play as were some prep school athletes," he writes in *Black College Sports.*

For example, four of the nine varsity players for Howard were players for the Twelfth Street YMCA club, the de facto champion club of the East Coast in 1910. One of the players for Howard during the 1910–11 season was Ed Gray, a third-team all-

American halfback at Amherst College in 1908. Gray entered Howard's medical school in 1909.

Today, National Collegiate Athletic Association rules would not permit someone in Gray's shoes to play after having suited up for four years as an undergraduate. It would be several years before schools began to create more stringent rules to govern student eligibility.

Rivalries between several of the historic black colleges flourished as basketball's popularity increased. One of the earliest rivalries was Howard versus Hampton Institute, a private coeducational college founded in 1868 by a twenty-seven-year-old Union general named Chapman Armstrong. During the 1911–12 season Hampton was boasting a modern sports facility, with 4,000 square feet of space and seating for 2,000. Howard dropped the game to Hampton in the new gym by a score of 19–16.

While colleges kept black America watching basketball, it wasn't the only source of action. Howard's second loss during the 1911–12 season was to the Monticello-Delaneys, a club team from the Pittsburgh area.

"The Monticello Basketball team of Pittsburgh defeated the champion Howard University team Friday, in Pittsburgh, by the score of 24–19," according to a March 14, 1912, story in the *New York Age*. "As this is Howard's third defeat in three years, the colored basketball world will be forced to recognize Monticello as one of the fastest colored quints. The Monticello team is open to meet all comers."

Monticello was a significant team because it had not lost for two years prior to beating Howard, and it was led by a dynamic player named Cumberland "Cum" W. Posey, Jr. He would become one of the most important men in black professional sports, especially baseball, during the first half of the twentieth century.

Born in 1891, Posey grew up in one of the largest homes in Homestead, Pennsylvania, and was from one of the most respected families in the region. According to Arthur Ashe, Posey's father was the first black man to be granted a chief engineer's license to operate a steamboat on the Mississippi River. The elder Posey also owned a coal boat company and a real estate business, and was a director of one of the largest banks in Homestead.

It was expected that Cum Posey would follow in his father's footsteps and manage one of the family businesses. But the athletically inclined Posey was interested in sports. He attended college in order to play the new game of basketball. "His admission to Penn State and acceptance on the varsity basketball team suggested a young man of stature, a good candidate to prove the equality of his race on the playing field of academe," Nelson George wrote.

It seems, however, that Posey was a better athlete than he was a student. He was forced off the team in 1909 because of academic ineligibility.

Because he was born into a financially secure family,

Posey was not driven to seek an education to better himself, as so many of his peers were doing at the time. For a while he drifted from college to college. He was spirited and adventurous. Some of that spirit is reflected in his life after he left the University of Pittsburgh, when he and his brother Seward organized the Monticello-Delaney Basketball Club.

Posey's all-star team was made up of some of the best black basketball players in the Pittsburgh area. They were also a pretty tough bunch of characters, according to a January 10, 1911, story in the *New York Age*. Monticello-Delaney played a game against the U.S. Army's 10th Cavalry Regiment, an all-black outfit that

Cum Posey organized the Monticello-Delaney Rifles, an all-star team made up of some of the best basketball players in the Pittsburgh area. [Francis C. Harris/The Amistad Pictorial History of the African American Athlete]

distinguished itself with Theodore Roosevelt in the Spanish-American War. The armed services had several teams in different sports, and the 10th Cavalry was also known to have an excellent baseball team.

"The boys in blue [10th Cavalry] proved as tricky as the horses they ride, and whenever an all-star player attempted to tackle a cavalryman by jumping on his back he was usually given a quick excursion through the air. . . . Medical aid and sticking plaster were called into use several times . . . but no one was seriously injured," the *New York Age* noted. There's no wonder the scores were low at that time. It took a lot of courage to shoot for a basket.

The fans were sometimes just as rowdy and impassioned as the players. In a game between the New York-based Incorporators and Orange, a team from New Jersey, a fan punched the captain of the Incorporators in the nose.

After the 1912 season, Cum Posey started a new team known as the Loendi Big Five, which was the dominant basketball team during the years before World War I. The players included Cum Posey, James "Stretch" Sessoms, William Young, William "Big Greasy" Bett, and James "Pappy" Ricks. Outside of Posey, who was 5 feet 9 inches tall and weighed 145 pounds, the team was made up of big men, fierce, strong, and agile. They played and practiced at the Pittsburgh Labor Temple, where pickup games were played regularly.

Unlike the teams of its day, the Loendi Big Five played a style of game that looks more like that of clubs of today. They were aggressive physically and were not afraid to rough up even the white teams they faced.

But they were also aggressive with the ball, playing a fast-paced game, running quickly downcourt, forcing turnovers, and taking lots of shots. It was a style of basketball that had not been seen before. There was also a financial reason for this, according to Arthur Ashe in *Long Road to Glory*: "Posey realized that boredom meant lower profits, so his team was aggressive."

The fans liked the up-tempo style and they flocked to the gate. More fans, more money.

Cum Posey, Jr., was said to be one of the best players to bounce a basketball down a court, but he will be remembered more for his contributions to baseball and the Negro Leagues. When he wasn't playing basketball, he could be found playing center field for the Murdock Grays, later to be renamed the Homestead Grays. Loendi could have grown into an even larger and more established team had Posey stuck with basketball, but he soon grew restless and turned to baseball full-time, first as a player, then as an owner/manager of the Homestead Grays.

Under the management of the Posey brothers, the Grays went on to become one of the greatest baseball teams in history, featuring such players as Josh Gibson, Leroy "Satchel" Paige, and Walter "Buck" Leonard.

Amateur clubs, colleges, and professionals like the Loendi Big Five continued to play each other during the first half of the 1900s. These games attracted the attention of fans because competition was fierce. For example, the powerful New York City-based St. Christopher's club was considered the best basketball team in the country during the 1913–14 season after they beat Howard University in front of 3,000 spectators in New York's Manhattan Casino.

Professionals for teams such as the Loendi Big Five and the Incorporators were paid a salary of approximately $25 a game, sometimes more. The professionalism is what began to get college officials and supporters

Posey (top left) was a star player for Duquesne University. [The Duquesne University Archives]

of amateur sports worried about the blurred lines between professional, collegiate, and scholastic teams. If one side was being paid outright, were the collegiate or scholastic players being paid under the table? It wasn't unheard of.

"There is . . . a place for the professional in basketball, but let him promote his own following and not try to feast upon the clientele of the legitimate amateur club," a writer for *Competitor,* a black monthly, commented. "There can be no middle ground between the amateur and the professional, nor can there be any contest of the two standards. The line draws itself, and the duty of each is plain."

Chapter 4

Black Colleges Unite

Despite the call for separation between the various levels of skill, scholastic, intercollegiate, and professional basketball teams played each other regularly. Hampton beat the Incorporators 24–15 to become the champions of the 1915–16 season. The Virginia school was a repeat champion the next season, with a YMCA team and two colleges—Lincoln University of Pennsylvania and Howard University—coming in second, third, and fourth.

Three years earlier, the first attempt had been made to create an athletic association of black schools and to apply a set of rules and regulations. A meeting was held at Hampton Institute on February 2, 1912, with representatives from Howard, Shaw University in North Carolina, Lincoln University, and Hampton. The participants formed the Colored Intercollegiate Athletic Association (CIAA).

Under the leadership of Ernest J. Marshall, a professor at Howard, the CIAA's primary goal was to unite the schools in a common effort to elevate athletics. "[The CIAA] will serve to train students in self-reliance and stimulate race-pride through athletic attainment," Marshall said.

In December 1913, several Southern schools followed suit. They held a meeting at Morehouse College in Atlanta, and formed the Southeastern Intercollegiate Athletic Conference (SIAC). The all-black schools included Fisk University (Nashville, Tennessee), Talladega (Alabama) College, Tuskegee Institute, Morehouse, Florida A&M, Knoxville (Tennessee) College, Jackson College, Morris Brown College in Atlanta, and Alabama State University.

In 1920, the Southwestern Athletic Conference (SWAC) was formed, consisting of five all-black colleges located in Texas: Prairie View A&M, Bishop College, Paul Quinn College, Wiley College, and Sam Houston College. Texas College joined the conference in 1922.

The conferences moved to make competition fairer by proposing that colleges who played against high schools and preparatory academies discontinue using professional players. According to historian Ocania Chalk, Howard University set the example by ceasing to allow students in the professional schools to become members of the school's varsity teams.

Despite the formation of the leagues, several schools, including Howard, continued to pay players. Then the conferences patterned their rules after the International

Olympic Committee (IOC), stating that in order for athletes to keep their amateur status they couldn't play any sport for money. Acceptance of pay constituted professionalism, and those athletes could no longer compete as amateurs.

Yet, schools kept paying players and competing against professional clubs well past World War I.

"There is a laxity among colored colleges in observing the rules of amateur sportsmanship, which, if continued, will commercialize college sports to such an extent as to cause them to lose their attractiveness," stated a February 9, 1924, editorial in the *New York Age*.

The editorial went on to scold Howard University for playing the Loendi Big Five that season, a game that Howard lost. The editorial went on to say, "The Pittsburgh team [Loendi] has played white professional teams and should not by any stretch of the imagination be considered amateurs. . . . The Colored Intercollegiate Athletic Association should have some law to check these violations."

The conference administrators tried to facilitate the growth of black college sports and legitimize the importance of varsity athletics. The conferences also tried to separate and regulate collegiate and professional basketball, but traditions and economics held the course. Essentially the conferences themselves were not strong enough to enforce the rules for the schools they supposedly governed.

One of the ways the conferences tried to encourage more intercollegiate play was to establish tourna ments and recognize championships. On February 8 and 9, 1925, four Atlanta schools—Morehouse, Clark University, Atlanta University, and Morris Brown College—held the first basketball tournament for black college teams in the South. On the first day, Morehouse, the school that Martin Luther King, Jr., would attend and play football for, pounded Morris Brown 48–18, while Atlanta squeaked by Clark 21–19. The next night, Morehouse won the tournament, beating Atlanta 37–13, making Morehouse the de facto black champion of the South.

As good as the men from Atlanta were, they were no match for their Northern rivals, especially Wilberforce University in Ohio. During the 1923–24 season, for example, Morehouse's only loss was to Wilberforce, 38–19.

During the 1920s, Morehouse and Wilberforce were two of the top teams in black college basketball. The third was Baltimore's Morgan College, a school that straddled the Mason-Dixon line—which separated the North and the South—and was able to recruit from both regions of the country.

While Baltimore had been a free city during slavery, there were slaves in Maryland. One of the most famous was Frederick Douglass, who escaped from slavery and became a leading abolitionist and newspaper publisher.

Before Charles Drew (top left) performed surgery, he performed on the courts, playing basketball at Dunbar High School in Washington, D.C. [Moorland-Spingarn Research Center, Howard University/Starlock Studio Collection, Archives Center, National Museum of American History]

Morgan College (now known as Morgan State University) was founded in 1867, the same year as Howard. Its equidistance to the industrial North and rural South probably contributed to Morgan's becoming a powerful force in basketball after World War I, with players such as Ed "Lanky" Jones, Talmadge Hill, Daniel "Pinky" Clark, and a bright young coach named Charles Drew.

After coaching at Morgan College, Drew went on to

graduate from McGill University Medical School in Montreal in 1933. Dr. Drew, a surgeon, is remembered most significantly for his work in the storage and use of blood plasma for transfusions, a process that saved the lives of millions during World War II and continues to save lives today. Very few people know what a terrific basketball player and coach Charles Drew was.

He began playing the game for Edwin Henderson at Washington, D.C.'s Dunbar High School, a championship school that is still a powerhouse today. Drew went on to letter in basketball, track, football, and soccer at Amherst College from 1923 to 1926. In 1923, he won the school's trophy for best all-around athlete.

There was already talk that Morgan could be the best team in the country the year Drew became their coach in 1927. He had inherited a great team with a reputation to uphold from their successful 1926 campaign. "It's not certain whether Wilberforce and Morgan will meet on the court this season, and it is not expected that Morehouse will encounter the Baltimore lads," wrote Thomas W. Young, in a March 6, 1926, story for the *Pittsburgh Courier.* "But if this triumvirate ever engages in a play-off, we harbor a very definite belief that Morgan will be the fittest. Morgan has a quint almost infallible. If the national championship has to be mythical this year, our unanimous vote is for Morgan College."

Everyone wondered whether the incoming coach

would be up to the challenge. Well, the numbers speak for themselves: an undefeated season and Morgan's 22–10 whipping of Hampton for the championship.

The problem of college teams playing professional clubs was still an issue deep into the 1920s. But by this time, the college teams were better trained, better coached, and were generally stronger than their pro rivals. The exception, though, was the Harlem Renaissance Big Five—known the world over as the Harlem Rens. They could match the talent of teams like Morgan.

"Coach Charlie Drew and his Morgan Bears journey

Dr. Drew is most famous for his work in the storage and use of blood plasma for transfusions, which saved millions of lives during World War II. [Brown Brothers]

to New York City tonight to do battle with the widely known and respected Renaissance Big Five," the *Pittsburgh Courier* heralded on March 18, 1927. "The Renaissance Casino will be the scene of what should be the biggest, fastest, and most exciting classic of the fast-waning [basketball] season."

The teams did not disappoint the fans. The Rens won 26–22. Coach Drew's Morgan Bears would lose a few more times to the Rens, before they would finally pick them off. On March 20, 1929, the Bears beat the Rens 41–40.

The black collegiate conferences were not happy when university teams and pro teams continued to play for what a lot of fans had come to consider a national championship.

"We are against an attempt down East to promote a Morgan College–Renaissance game," wrote Fay Young in a February 18, 1928, editorial in the *Chicago Defender.* "We would be against Hampton, Lincoln or Howard playing the Loendi of Pittsburgh and we are against any college playing a pro team. It professionalizes the whole team the minute they play in open competition against professionals even if they are only semiprofessionals."

Why did the schools resist regulations? Some historians believe it was based on revenue. The college and pro basketball championship games drew thousands of paying spectators and served as an excellent advertise-

"Everybody who was anybody" came to see the Harlem Renaissance team play. [UPI/Corbis-Bettmann]

ment for the college's academic-program recruitment. It gave the alumni something to feel proud of and therefore they were more willing to make contributions.

Others claim the resistance was caused by the "black Renaissance attitude," a growing awareness and pride that had spread throughout the black community. As early as 1920, poets, writers, artists, musicians, and educators had begun redefining what it meant to be black in America. They drew their pain on broad sweeps of canvas; they danced and sang about their indignities on stages from Paris to Peru. These young black intellectuals and artists set their goals based on self-confidence and self-esteem. This spirited period in African-American history was emerging in cities across the country—Chicago, St. Louis, Detroit, Boston, Philadelphia, Baltimore, and Washington, D.C. But it was strongest in New York City, where this rebirth and renewal of the Negro spirit was centered and from which this period got its name: the Harlem Renaissance. This time of new attitudes, self-pride, and racial dignity gave rise to a kind of independence that spilled over into sports. Young blacks were no longer content to imitate whites or follow rules that weren't in their best interest.

The Rens were to Harlem what baseball's Dodgers were to Brooklyn. When the Rens held court, everybody who was anybody came to see them play. It was a matter of pride. To play against them was considered an honor, and college athletic directors weren't willing to give up that prestige or that opportunity.

For whatever reasons black colleges insisted upon playing professional teams, the debate never ended. It was an annual issue that the CIAA and black colleges would wrestle with for years to come. As for the Rens, their professionalism and excellence on the court made them the best basketball team in America—black or white.

Chapter 5

The Harlem Rens

According to some historians, if there is someone who deserves the title of Godfather of black basketball it is Robert L. "Bob" Douglas. As the owner of the Rens, Douglas created a black professional team that earned the respect of players and fans, both white and black. The Rens were the best of the best.

Douglas was born and raised in Saint Kitts, British West Indies. In 1901, as a young man, he moved to New York. His first job was as a doorman, where he earned $22 a month.

"I saw my first basketball game on 52nd Street and Tenth Avenue in 1903," Douglas was quoted as saying in Art Rust's *Illustrated History of the Black Athlete.* "I came from St. Kitts . . . and soccer was the game played there. But when I saw that basketball game, I thought it was the most remarkable game ever."

Douglas, along with two others, started a Caribbean athletic club called the Spartan Field Club. The club formed a variety of sports teams, including cricket and basketball. They played against other black clubs in New York City, such as St. Philip's Church, the Alphas Club, St. Christopher's, and Salem Church.

The Spartans played basketball in the Metropolitan Basketball Association, which was made up of teams in the New York area, but they also played clubs like the Loendi Five and the Chicago-based Forty Club. The Spartans had quite a successful amateur team, but near the end of 1921 the Metropolitan Basketball Association, which was against professionalism in amateur basketball, cited them for a violation. "They directed us to release Frank Forbes and Leon Monde because they'd played sports for money during the summer months," Douglas said. "We ignored the association and, by doing this, they accused the Spartans of threatening to wreck the organization." Douglas felt he could make a lot of money if he organized a professional team. So, he created the Rens.

By 1923, Douglas had approached William Roche, another West Indian, who had made his living selling real estate in Harlem. Roche had opened a two-story entertainment center in 1922 called the Harlem Renaissance Casino. The Casino showed first-run movies on the first floor and had a ballroom available for dancing and banquets on the second floor. The Renaissance Casino's ballroom was also large enough to play basketball in.

Douglas and Roche pounded out a deal by which

Douglas's team would be called the Harlem Renaissance and would play their home games in the ballroom. But it wasn't an easy sell at first. When Douglas first asked Roche about the idea, Roche's initial reaction had been "No." Roche was worried about the "rough" crowds that followed basketball teams during the twenties.

"But I guaranteed him we wouldn't do any damage to his ballroom," Douglas said. "Since it was a new place . . . I told him the team would give the place publicity, and I'd name the team the Renaissance, although I didn't like the name." Douglas wanted to keep the

Robert L. "Bob" Douglas was the owner, coach, promoter, and organizer of the Rens. [Naismith Memorial Basketball Hall of Fame]

The Rens played ball right on the Harlem Renaissance Casino's slippery ballroom floor. [© Donna Mussenden Van Der Zee]

name Spartans, from his old club, but Roche didn't like that name.

The two entrepreneurs went back and forth, give and take. But the icebreaker of the deal was a financial one. "I told [Roche] he'd make lots of money with his percentage of the gates," Douglas said. Roche seemingly didn't need any more encouragement.

The Rens played their first game in the Harlem Renaissance Casino on November 30, 1923, and beat the Chicago Collegians 28–22.

As was typical of the era, games were played right on the ballroom's dance floor, with two portable baskets set up and portable wooden chairs on either side for the fans. The court was small, approximately 60 feet long and 35 feet wide. According to Nelson George, "Under a chandelier beneath which big bands played, the Rens took set shots and tried not to scuff up the floor too much.

"All you had to worry about was running into that hard wooden barrier around the floor because it had sharp edges. Sometimes when the game got rough, the guys would be flying over that barrier into people's laps."

William "Pop" Gates, one of the Rens' biggest stars in the 1930s and 1940s, said the floor was very slippery. "They had baskets that they put up before every ball game and markers they put down for the foul lines and so forth," Gates said in an interview in *Cages to Jump Shots.* "The spectators were seated at tables in loges in the second tier and in boxes in the third tier. That was supposed to be an elite area."

Despite the problems with the Renaissance Casino, the Rens didn't have any problems on the court. With Douglas as manager and Eric Illidge as coach/road manager, the Rens won 2,318 games and lost only 381 in 26 seasons.

The first Rens club featured Harold Slocum (who would remain the team's captain until 1932), Frank Forbes, Harold Mayers, Zack Anderson, Hy Monte, and Leon Monte. In later years, Douglas said the key

In 26 seasons, the Renaissance won 2,318 games and lost only 381.
[© Donna MussendenVan Der Zee]

to the Rens' success was having a team-oriented offense and a quick defense.

In the 1920s the game was still tough, but there were more fouls and penalty calls. Players were beginning to practice their shooting techniques rather than depending solely upon stopping the other team from scoring. "When we played, you had to check your man," Gates told Nelson George. "Make him take two steps to get one. Nobody guards nobody now. . . . When we played you had to earn your grits."

In 1924, the Rens moved into the position of respect

the Loendi team had once held. The Pittsburgh power club was not as strong as it had once been. It was a sign that Douglas's ideas of playing tough offense as a team was winning out over Posey's rough and running defense. As good as the Rens were becoming on the court, however, basketball was still not as popular as baseball and, for the most part, games became social events, where people came to see who was with whom and what they were wearing.

"We had to have a dance afterwards or nobody would come to the [game]," Eyre Saitch, who played for the Rens in the 1930s, told Arthur Ashe. "[T]he Renaissance . . . was right across the street from The Red Rooster [nightclub] . . . If you didn't get there by seven o'clock, you didn't get in the . . . door. The big game didn't start until 10 o'clock."

Pretty late at night for a basketball game, but having the social atmosphere for basketball made it possible for teams to attract the crowds. Saitch told Ashe that the Rens' players made between $800 and $1,000 a month. Not much by today's standards, but at that time a nickel bought a loaf of bread and an apartment rented for $60 a month.

According to Ashe, "They more than earned their pay since they were on the road 75 percent of the time." The Rens played 150 games per year against clubs, YMCA teams, and colleges. The Rens were a tough group on the floor, but management was even tougher off the floor. Illidge is said to have carried a gun and would not let his club touch the ball until he had their share of the gate profits in their hands. Illidge demanded cash—no checks.

Every year in the spring the Rens played black college teams in the South. It was during one of these trips that the Rens were almost involved in a serious riot.

Unlike in baseball, where a serious color line had been drawn, basketball games between black and white teams, at least in the North, were fairly commonplace. Fans didn't seem to mind all-white teams playing against all-black teams, but integrated teams were not acceptable. Some white colleges continued to use black players, but the numbers were low. One of the Rens' great rivals was the Original Celtics, also a New York team. Later the Celtics, now in Boston, would become one of basketball's greatest teams. The South Philadelphia Hebrew Association played against the Rens on the court and all three clubs respected each other off the court as well.

This respect for each other, however, wasn't always shared by the spectators who watched their games. During a game in Louisville, Kentucky, the Rens were surprised to see members of the Celtics—including their coach, Joe Lapchick—sitting in the stands.

"Joe Lapchick, who knew our center Tarzan Cooper, ran out on the court and embraced Cooper because he was so glad to see him," Douglas recalls. "This was Jim

Though Joe Lapchick (top right) and the Original Celtics were one of the Rens' greatest rivals, the two teams respected each other on and off the court. [Underwood & Underwood/Corbis-Bettmann]

Crow country, and the races were strictly separated. The Celtic players were put out of their hotel and a riot was narrowly averted."

Like their brothers in baseball, the Rens had more than their fair share of tough times on the road. Despite having an air-conditioned bus with reclining seats to travel in, going to places in the South and Midwest meant driving 250 and 300 miles at a stretch because no hotels would allow them to rent rooms.

They were confronted by racism and discrimination along the way. NO COLORED signs met them at doors to restaurants and restrooms. They often ate cold sandwiches on the bus and slept on hard benches in gyms and churches. Eyre Saitch said that the team occasionally slept in prisons because hotels wouldn't put them up. "[W]e'd spray the bedbugs before we went out to play and they'd be dead when we got back. . . . We sometimes had over a thousand dollars in our pockets and we couldn't get a good . . . meal."

The team had to change clothes on the bus, too, because the players were not allowed to go into white dressing rooms. "We weren't alone. All of us [African-American] ball players were treated that way."

Frank Baid, a star for the Indianapolis Kautskys, said he was sympathetic to the plight of the Rens when they were on the road. "When the Renaissance came in, they had to stay at the colored YMCA at Sennet and Michigan [streets]," he says in *Cages to Jump Shots*. "We'd go out with them and play around the state. There was no place they could get anything to eat, so they brown-bagged it. We'd get to the gym at 6 or 6:30 for an 8 o'clock game, and they'd be down in the locker room already dressed and having a sandwich or something. Maybe they'd save part of it to eat on the way back to Indianapolis. I thought that was one of the most unfair things. They were nice guys and they were tough. I'm sure over the years they beat us more than we beat them."

It didn't get any better on the court, according to Pop Gates. "Many times when we played in the South, we'd have to fight our way in and out of the arenas," he told authors Art and Edna Rust. "One time in Marion, Ohio, [Clarence] 'Puggy' Bell went into the crowd scrambling for a ball and a woman kicked him from behind. One time in Cicero, Illinois, where we were playing, a fight broke out. The lights went out and when they came back on, twelve of us were in the middle of the floor with chairs in our hands. Then another time in Indianapolis, Indiana, some white guy kept yelling nigger-this and nigger-that. After we picked out who was yelling, I conveniently missed a Puggy Bell pass and the basketball knocked the guy right off his chair. We did that a lot of times."

The Rens didn't let the racism get them down—they got even by playing the best game they could. Puggy Bell, who joined the Rens in 1938, earned the reputation for being one of the best long jump shooters playing the game. He gave credit to the whole team, saying they were "so good we'd spot clubs ten points, with the racists officiating taken into account. At that time we had a policy not to beat a team by more than ten points. In other words, hold the score down so we could come back and play them again. Don't show the other team up so bad they wouldn't play us again. After all, we had to make money."

One of the few teams the Rens didn't spot 10 points

was their best rival, the Original Celtics. In 1925, the Rens played the Celtics six times, with each team winning three. It was through these games that the Rens earned a great deal of respect in the basketball world. But it wasn't enough to win over the founders of the American Basketball League (ABL). An invitation to join the league went out to the Celtics, the best white team, but not the Rens, the best black pro team. Joining the ABL would have meant more money, but Joe Lapchick, the player-coach-manager of the Celtics, declined to join, partly because black players and teams were excluded.

"This snub of blacks came in the same year the National Football League began to ease its black players from its member teams," Arthur Ashe wrote. "But, like the best white major-league baseball squads, the best white professional teams actually sought out confrontations against the premier black aggregations. These interracial games virtually guaranteed a jammed box office."

The rivalry between the Celtics and the Rens drew thousands of fans. In 1929, the Celtics beat the Rens 38–31 in front of 10,000 people who packed the 21st Regiment Armory in New York City to see the game. But the Rens would win their first mythical "World Championship" in 1932, defeating their rivals in a two-game series: 37–34 on March 30 and 30–23 on April 3.

(The World Professional Basketball tournaments didn't begin until 1939.)

In 1933 the Rens won an incredible 88 games in a row. But a year to the day later, the Celtics broke the Rens' winning streak and won a one-point victory to reclaim the "world" title. Crowds of up to 15,000 would flock to see the Celtics and Rens fight it out on the court. But even more gratifying was the teams' respect for each other after the game.

From 1932 to 1936 the Rens, featuring a lineup of future Hall of Famer Tarzan Cooper, "Wee" Willie Smith, James "Pappy" Ricks, Eyre Saitch, Johnny Holt, and Bill Yancey, achieved a record of 473 wins and 49 losses.

As strategies and player techniques changed because of teams like the Loendi Big Five, the Original Celtics, Morgan College, and the Renaissance Big Five, so did the rules that governed the game. The changes began in 1932, about the same time the Rens and Celtics were tearing up the basketball world. The 10-second rule, which forced the offense to quickly get the ball past midcourt, was introduced. The first three-second lane violation (a player with the ball could not stand and hold the ball for more than three seconds in the foul-shot lane) was set in place, as well. These changes forced players to pass and shoot more often, resulting in a faster-paced game and higher scoring, with an emphasis on teamwork.

In 1936, the three-second rule was amended further to include every player in the lane, forcing players to move even faster. "Blacks particularly liked this innovation because the fancy passing that ensued was entertaining as well as productive," Ashe wrote. "Now, all ten players were constantly in motion, juggling for position and looking for fakes and picks. [A pick is set by standing firmly in front of a defender to temporarily block him from your teammate with the ball.] The fans loved it and an added premium was placed on compatibility."

In 1937, the center jump after each basket was eliminated and the "race horse" maneuver was invented. The offense would inbound the ball to a teammate, who would either pass it to another teammate streaking toward the basket, or streak toward the basket himself for an easy layup.

"In those days . . . we played by halves and then changed to fifteen-minute quarters," Eyre Saitch told Arthur Ashe. "The referees only called flagrant fouls . . . with no jump balls, we just outran everybody."

The year 1937 also saw another attempt at an organized professional basketball league, this time the National Basketball League (NBL). Just as its predecessor, the American Basketball League, had done a decade earlier, the NBL declined to allow black squads to play. It was another slap in the face to the Rens, who had time and again proven themselves to be the top basketball team in the country, black or white.

The Rens were steadfast, though, and continued to build on their winning ways. Despite the snub from the NBL, the Rens went on to win the first World Professional Basketball Tournament in 1939. The Rens downed the Oshkosh (Wisconsin) All Stars 34–25 at Chicago Stadium. This was the kind of recognition that Douglas had sought all along—an official, out-right championship where black and white professional teams played each other for the title. Each Rens player

"Tarzan" Cooper, "Wee" Willie Smith, James "Pappy" Ricks, Eyre Saitch, Johnny Holt, and Bill Yancey proved a good Ren lineup, achieving a record of 473 wins between 1932 and 1936. [Todd Bolten]

was given $1,000 for the victory. But the recognition meant more.

ame before Bob Douglas bought Gates's contract from the Yankees for a couple of hundred dollars. He then signed Gates to a contract worth $124 a month.

first world professional basketball tournament on record. The victory in Chicago was one of the team's greatest achievements. The Rens had brought full realization to the world that they were the best."

the war had forced the team to cut down on its barnstorming. Also, players were drafted or voluntarily joined the war effort.

Many of the Rens players took up weekend residence in Washington, D.C. Although under a different name, the old Rens, now called the Washington Bears, won the World Professional Basketball Tournament, again at Chicago Stadium, in front of 12,000 people. They beat the Oshkosh All-Stars (again) 43–31. The Rens began hitting the road as the war came to an end, but they weren't the same power they once had been.

This could have been the last hurrah for the team, except that in 1947 something extraordinary happened. Jack "Jackie" Roosevelt Robinson, following an apprenticeship in the minor leagues, joined the Brooklyn Dodgers, becoming the first African American to play major-league baseball in the twentieth century.

That opened the door for all sports to integrate. The following year "Mike Duffey, president of the white National Basketball League, asked [the Rens] to replace the Detroit Vagabond Kings' franchise, which had lasted until mid-December and then folded," Douglas told Art Rust. Although it was a tremendous sports breakthrough, Jackie Robinson and baseball were getting most of the press. This basketball move didn't make headlines in most newspapers.

The Rens, representing Dayton, Ohio, were called the Dayton Rens. Douglas added that he did not want Dayton as a home court, but had to use it because of league insistence. The fans of Dayton didn't really accept the team as theirs, and they refused to attend games.

The 1948 Dayton Rens were led by player-coach Pop Gates. "Despite lack of size, a lot of our players being over the hill, a thin bench . . . our club—the only *all-black franchise* in the history of major league sports—built a competitive 14–26 record," Douglas said, but unfortunately it was the team's last season.

For their important role in early basketball and their team accomplishments, the Renaissance Big Five was named to the Naismith Memorial Basketball Hall of Fame in 1963. Bob Douglas, their owner, helped pave the way for black professional competition and an increased awareness of basketball in the community at large.

For his efforts, Douglas was named to the Hall of Fame in 1971.

Chapter 6

The Globetrotters

If there is anything that can excite a basketball crowd, it's fancy passing and dribbling. And no other team does it better than the Harlem Globetrotters performing in the magical circle—all the players on the team in a circle making trick passes behind the back, over the shoulder, between the legs to the music of "Sweet Georgia Brown."

While the Rens were tearing up the East Coast in the 1920s and 1930s, the Globetrotters became synonymous, ironically, with Chicago. The irony being that the Globetrotters are often mistaken for a team that was founded and based in Harlem.

The Globetrotters began much the same way as the Rens, from an existing basketball club: the Savoy Big Five of Chicago, which itself was an outgrowth of two other teams (the Giles Post, a Negro American Legion team, and Wendell Phillips High School). They played their games at the Savoy Ballroom in Chicago.

The man who first saw the potential for a profes-

Abe Saperstein (pictured here with Tom "Tarzan" Spencer) organized what would eventually come to be regarded as one of history's best basketball teams, the Harlem Globetrotters. [AP/Wide World]

sional, money-making venture was Abe Saperstein, a white social worker turned businessman. The Rens had proved that an all-black basketball team could make money barnstorming. The Savoy team was managed by Dick Hudson, a former football star. Each player was paid $27 per game. Saperstein assumed control of the team in 1926, though it's a little fuzzy how this happened.

In *Elevating the Game*, Nelson George quotes Tommy Brookins, a forward on the Savoy club, as saying that the team name was originally Tommy Brookins' Globetrotters, then changed to the Original Chicago Globetrotters.

Saperstein, Brookins said, was brought in by Hudson because, as a white man, Saperstein would be better able to book games in places like Wisconsin and Minnesota. Saperstein promised the team that he would get them 10 games in exchange for $100 and 10 percent of the gate.

The first game was against a team from Hinckley, Illinois, located about 20 miles west of Chicago, on January 7, 1927. The 'Trotters won, and the team made $75.

Saperstein not only booked those 10 games, but secretly, according to Brookins, he booked another 10. The original team featured a nucleus of Walter "Toots" Wright, Byron "Fat" Long, Willis "Kid" Oliver, Al "Runt" Pullins, and Andy Washington. "In fact, [Saperstein] committed them to so many contests that he decided to organize another team, which he labeled the Harlem Globetrotters, to fulfill these obligations," George writes. "Within a few months of Saperstein's involvement, the Chicago Trotters disbanded."

Despite his success with the Harlem Globetrotters, Saperstein was not trusted by a number of blacks associated with basketball. A theory accepted by the black press at the time had Saperstein allegedly making arrangements with white team owners to keep blacks out of the Basketball Association of America, which was formed in 1946, so that he would have the pick of the best black players.

So Saperstein's involvement with the early 'Trotters is looked at with both fondness and disdain. What is certain, though, is that Saperstein organized the Harlem Globetrotters to capitalize on the area in New York City associated with black class and style and to put them in the same league as the Rens.

Saperstein served as the team's general manager, coach, and trainer. He drove the car to the games and served as the team's only substitute. In the early days of the team, the Globetrotters were guaranteed $25 and half the gate receipts. Later the guaranteed fee was upped to $75— Saperstein got $20 per game; each player received $10 plus $5 for expenses.

Just as the Rens had to endure tough conditions on the road because of racism, so did the 'Trotters. In Shelby, Montana, for example, gamblers threatened to shoot the team if they won, and the sheriff threatened to shoot the team if they lost. The Globetrotters won the game and had to steal out of town in their uniforms with their clothes under their arms. Often the team had to sleep in the car, an old Model T, because they couldn't find any other place.

The team's "clowning" didn't come to pass until well after the team had established itself as competition for the Rens. In 1940, the Globetrotters won the world championship in Chicago, beating the Rens 37–36 in

Globetrotters alumnus Nat "Sweetwater" Clifton became one of the first black men to play in the NBA. [UPI/Corbis-Bettmann]

the quarter finals and the Chicago Bruins in the finals, 31-29. It wasn't supposed to have happened that way.

The 'Trotters were invited to the tournament to fill out the first round. The organizers thought they would be entertaining and fun, but hardly in the same league with the other teams.

The clowning and antics of the Globetrotters came about as a way to rest the players, who were on the road much of the time wrestling fatigue and tough conditions. According to team lore, the first "official" act of entertainment came about by happenstance in a cold gym in Iowa. In was so cold that the court was ringed with potbellied stoves. Willis "Kid" Oliver leaned back into a stove and his shorts caught fire. He ran screaming onto the court, his pants smoldering. He stopped play and the audience, which was predominantly white, laughed at the scene.

While many have enjoyed the antics of the Globetrotters over the years, more than a few black historians and writers have found the whole routine demeaning to the race. The theory is that the Globetrotters acted silly because few whites would accept an all-black basketball team completely dominating an all-white team, so they were forced to act foolish in order to avoid confrontations. There was also an economic reason: who wants to play a team that comes in, beats you up, takes the money, and leaves?

The routines, however, played into the stereotypes that many white people had about black people, and were opposite to what the Rens (and many Negro League baseball owners and players) were trying to do: create a professional image. To add insult to injury, the 'Trotters were run by a white man, making Saperstein's actions look opportunistic and condescending rather than benevolent.

Regardless of Saperstein's intentions and the players' clowning, the Globetrotters were a team to be reckoned with. Making the team was akin to surviving boot camp. In the 1940s, the Globetrotters were headquartered at the Evans Hotel, on Chicago's South Side. Players invited to training camp could expect to compete against 100 hopeful candidates to fill spots on the "A" (or Eastern) squad or on the "B" teams that played in the West and South, or to get a place on one of the traveling opposition teams.

How tough was the competition? Meadowlark Lemon, one of the most athletic, gifted, and comedic men to play the game, described the tryouts: "I saw all those young guys flying, and I mean flying, through the air, slam-dunking, rebounding, dribbling, shooting long jump shots, doing everything spectacular. It looked like a waterfall of balls going through the baskets."

Those who survived training camp had to relearn the game of basketball. They had to learn the "'Trotter Way" of playing the game.

Connie Hawkins (number 42) starred with the Phoenix Suns, but got his start with the Harlem Globetrotters. [AP/Wide World]

The center position on the 'Trotters was the key to winning basketball games, as well as winning the hearts of fans, just as on all the good teams during that era.

"From a position in the high post area near the top of the key the center told jokes, made funny faces and sounds, and starred in most of the reams [skits], from shifting suddenly into baseball to throwing water on the referees," according to Nelson George.

In fact, several of the Globetrotters had baseball experience. Reece "Goose" Tatum played baseball for the Indianapolis Clowns and basketball for the 'Trotters. The Indianapolis Clowns would perform between innings.

"[Tatum and King Tut] would go through a tooth-pulling act where Goose was a dentist and Tut was a patient," says Othello Renfroe, a former Negro League player. "Tut would fill up his mouth with corn. Goose would try to pull the tooth but without success. Then he'd put a firecracker in Tut's mouth and when it exploded [safely] Tut would spit out the corn like he was spitting teeth. They kept you in stitches."

Tatum, who stood 6 feet 6 inches tall and weighed 190 pounds, played for the 'Trotters from 1942 to 1955, alongside Lemon and Marques Haynes, who was deservedly billed as the "World's Greatest Dribbler."

The 'Trotters didn't have traditional guards like other teams in that era. With the center in the high post and a forward in one corner, the other three players shifted and weaved in undefinable but no-less-skilled positions. They dribbled with finesse and made incredible passes with deft accuracy.

The 'Trotters were able to attract some of the best black talent in the country, including more than a few young men who went on to play in the National Basketball Association (NBA). One of these young men was Wilt "The Stilt" Chamberlain.

Chamberlain, who stands 7 feet 1 inch tall and weighs 275 pounds, is a native of Philadelphia and was celebrated as both a prep school and college athlete. In fact, he is responsible for changing the out-of-bounds rule in college basketball. While Chamberlain was at the University of Kansas (1954–57), his teammates

would throw the inbound pass over the backboard.
Chamberlain would jump up over the man guarding
him, catch the ball after it cleared the backboard, and
put it through the hoop.

Chamberlain left Kansas after his junior year and
joined the Globetrotters before signing with the
Philadelphia Warriors in 1959.

Nat "Sweetwater" Clifton, one of the first black men
to play in the NBA, and Connie Hawkins, who starred

*Wilt Chamberlain played ball as a Globetrotter before signing on with the
Philadelphia Warriors in 1959. While playing with the Warriors, he scored
100 points in a game against the New York Knickerbockers on March 2,
1962. [AP/Wide World]*

with the Phoenix Suns, are two more examples of b-ballers who got their professional start with the Harlem Globetrotters.

The 'Trotters still play basketball, although they are now best known for their entertaining style. No longer do they compete for world championships, although the members of the team could probably give most teams in the NBA a run for their money.

The Globetrotters have truly been global over the years, playing for such dignitaries as the Pope and in such faraway places as China, showing off their talents and thrilling fans with acrobatic stunts. The players are considered goodwill ambassadors and are as dignified off the court as they are talented on it.

Chapter 7

White Colleges, Black Players

While professional sports in this country had yet to come to grips with the idea of blacks and whites playing on the same team before Jackie Robinson crossed the color barrier in baseball in 1947, several white Northern colleges had long before decided to break that barrier.

Schools such as Harvard, Beloit, Amherst, Oberlin, Ohio Wesleyan, and other institutions had a long history of integrated athletic teams. This is not to say that all white Northern colleges were so enlightened. Princeton had a whites-only policy for varsity athletics until 1944. And being a black player at one of those schools didn't mean that you were instantly accepted.

In *Black College Sport*, Ocania Chalk explains that life for black athletes at white colleges was difficult. While the facilities were much better than their counterparts at black colleges, African-American athletes had to be almost twice as good as white players and often found themselves shut out of social activities because they were either the only or one of the few blacks on campus. "Why, it was thought, should a college that was overwhelmingly white display a mediocre or ordinary black athlete? If the play was less than outstanding, it was just as well that it should be wrapped in white skin," Chalk wrote.

This didn't mean that black hoopsters were timid on the court. An article in *The New York Times* in 1919 described an on-court tussle between John Howard Johnson, a big, burly center and Columbia University's first black basketball player, and a white guard from the University of Pennsylvania. That same year, another black athlete had his name splashed across the sports page of *The New York Times*: "Robeson Leads Attack— Rutgers Easily Beats West Virginia by 44 to 22."

Paul Leroy Robeson was born on April 9, 1898, in Somerville, New Jersey. The son of William Drew Robeson, a minister in the African Methodist Episcopal Church, and Maria Louise Bustill, Robeson excelled in sports and academics and was an accomplished singer in the church choir.

Robeson entered Rutgers, a New Jersey state university, on an academic scholarship in 1917. He immediately made his mark as an athlete and a student. But, as with a number of black college players at white schools, acceptance, much less success, didn't come as easily.

At 6 feet 3 inches tall and weighing over 200 pounds, Robeson looked to be a big plus for the football and

Paul Robeson made his mark at Rutgers as an athlete and a student before he became an accomplished singer and actor. [AP/Wide World]

basketball teams. But several players on his football team said they would quit before they played with Robeson or any other African American.

Robeson experienced some of the most brutal treatment at Rutgers at the hands of his own teammates. During his first day of scrimmage he suffered a broken nose, a dislocated shoulder, and a split eyebrow.

Robeson finally got fed up one day, the day his teammates realized they could no longer push him around. "The next play came right at my defensive end position; the whole backfield came at me," Robeson told Ralph Edwards in *Paul Robeson: His Political Legacy to the Twentieth-Century Gladiator*. Robeson, in a rage, swept aside the blockers, knocking them over like dolls. "Then there was only the ball carrier; I wanted to kill him," Robeson said. "I actually had him up above my head . . . I was going to smash him so hard to the ground that . . . he'd break right in two."

The coach immediately put him on the varsity squad, where he was named to the all-American team in 1917 and 1918. During his four years at Rutgers, Robeson won 13 varsity letters in football, basketball, baseball, and track. In his junior year, he was elected to Phi Beta Kappa, the country's most well-known and respected academic honor fraternity.

Despite his success, Robeson could not live on campus; and although he was an excellent singer, Robeson was not allowed to join the school choir or glee club.

But some of his classmates must have respected his talents and contributions to the university. A verse in the school's 1919 yearbook reads: "All hats off to Robey, All honors to his name. On the diamond, court, or football field, He's brought old Rutgers fame."

Black stars at white colleges would continue to emerge during the 1920s and 1930s. One of those star basketball players was George Gregory, Jr., who played center for Columbia University from 1927 to 1931. Gregory was born in New York City in 1906. He dropped out of high school for several years, but was persuaded by Leonard Palmer, coach of the DeWitt

Despite being elected to Phi Beta Kappa and winning 13 varsity letters in football, basketball, baseball, and track, Paul Robeson was not allowed to live on campus or join the school choir. [Rutgers Archives]

Only the second black person ever to play for Columbia University, George Gregory led his basketball team to win the 1930 league title and was named captain of the team for the 1930–31 season. [AP/Wide World]

Clinton High School basketball team, to come back to school. Gregory graduated in 1927 and enrolled at Columbia.

During the 1928–29 season, he played for the varsity squad, the second black to do so. He scored 155 points in 17 games, ranking fourth in scoring in the Ivy League. The next season, he moved up to second in league scoring by popping in 168 points in 22 games. He averaged more than 7.6 points per game at a time when most teams scored around 30 points per game.

Gregory's playing helped guide Columbia to the

league title in 1930. "Columbia Quintet Wins League Title—10,000 See Contest—Gregory Is Star of Game," a March 12, 1930, *New York Times* headline announced.

One of the highest honors a player can receive is to be named captain of the team. Gregory earned that honor for the 1930–31 season.

Columbia retained the league title that season. Gregory averaged 8.3 points per game, and scored one of the more memorable baskets in Columbia history in a game against Cornell. "[Gregory] was guarded from behind by Schroeder, so he flipped in the basket from about ten feet out on an overhead toss with his back to basket," *The New York Times* announced.

In January 1934, the University of Michigan, perhaps unintentionally, forced the issue of racism and discrimination when Franklin Lett was dismissed from the freshman squad. Coach F. C. Cappon told Lett that there had never been a black basketball player in the Big Ten, and that there had been an agreement among the league's coaches that there would never be.

Roy Wilkins, assistant secretary of the National Association for the Advancement of Colored People, replied in anger that Cappon's remarks were an insult to black Americans. Lett was allowed back on the team, but he was never allowed to play varsity basketball.

What made this whole ordeal odd was that Michigan didn't discriminate in other varsity sports. Eddie Tolan starred in track for Michigan and went on to win two gold medals at the 1932 Olympic Games in Los Angeles.

In 1933, it looked as if the University of Wisconsin was going to break the color barrier. Forward John Watts led his high school team to two state titles and was named to the all-state squad. Dr. Walter E. Meanwell, coach of the Badgers, saw Watts play and said he was the "finest prospect the State has ever turned out." When asked if Watts would be allowed to compete for Wisconsin, Meanwell—who had coached the Badgers since the end of World War I—said that Watts would be given every consideration to make the varsity team. "There is no reason why a colored boy should not play basketball," Meanwell said. "They compete in football and track and basketball is no different. Any boy will get a fair chance to make my team, regardless of color. Watts is a fine prospect, and I'd like to see him enter Wisconsin." Watts never made it, and it is unclear if he played college basketball anywhere.

James Meelix, an all-state forward from Columbus, Ohio, was denied a chance to play for his state university. Ohio State coach Macea Hill told Meelix that he wouldn't get past the freshman squad. Even white newspapers and magazines commented on the ridiculousness of shutting black athletes out of basketball.

"A sport in which the Negro undeniably excels is basketball," wrote Curt Riess for *Esquire* magazine in 1941. "Although the sport is continued mainly in high schools and colleges, [the black athlete] rarely has a chance to play except in the colored colleges. The courts of the Big Ten are closed to him, in spite of the fact that there have been such great colored basketball stars as Sidat-Singh [Syracuse University], George Gregory [Columbia], and William King [Long Island University]."

Black colleges had been keeping up, albeit in segregated leagues. The majority of the activity in black college basketball centered around the CIAA. Its two best teams were the long-dominant Morgan College Bears from Baltimore and the upstart Virginia Union Panthers from Richmond.

During the 1937–38 season, Virginia Union's coach, Henry Huckles, recruited some of the best available student-athletes and made a run at Morgan. The teams finished tied for the league title that season, and Virginia Union won its first championship the following year. In March 1940, Virginia Union would go on to prove that it was the league's top team by beating an all-star selection of the CIAA's best, 54–51.

Black sportswriters, upset about the shutting out of black players in the Big Ten and of black teams in the National Invitational Tournament (NIT), which determined the national champion among white schools, saw the enormous potential to strike a blow against racism by having Virginia Union play a white college team.

Their wish came true when Virginia Union defeated

Brooklyn College 54–38 in New York City. "They moved like lightning and acted like they knew what was going on at all times," Brooklyn coach Artie Musciant said after the 1941 game. "They were in wonderful shape and played like champions."

In the next season, North Carolina State, a black college from Durham, won the CIAA title. They went on to beat Brooklyn 37–34.

Black sportswriters campaigned to have at least one black college invited to the NIT in 1942. But Ned Irish, the tournament's organizer, invited only the best

Before he broke the color barrier in baseball, Jackie Robinson was a four-sport athlete at the UCLA and the Pacific Coast Conference's leading scorer. [Metro Media TV, National Baseball Hall of Fame]

white colleges of the day: Long Island University, Rhode Island State, Toledo University, West Kentucky State, West Virginia, and Creighton University. Toledo had two black players, Dave Minor and Emlen Tunnell, who aided their team to a fourth-place finish.

World War II helped push along blacks at white colleges as coaches filled their teams with the best available talent. Jackie Robinson, who would go on to break the color barrier in baseball, was a phenomenal four-sport athlete at the University of California Los Angeles (UCLA) during the early 1940s. In basketball he was the Pacific Coast Conference's leading scorer, and in football he was its leading ground gainer.

Schools and conferences that had long closed their doors to black athletes began to open up. Princeton's first black player was Arthur Wilson, who was also honorary captain of the team. In 1943, Dick Culberson, a transfer from Virginia Union College (a CIAA school) suited up for Iowa to become the first black player on a varsity squad in the Big Ten.

"The racial logjam was finally broken during the five years from 1946 to 1950," wrote Arthur Ashe. "Joe Louis, Jackie Robinson, Althea Gibson, and Jesse Owens left such positive impressions upon their respective sports that the entire American sports establishment felt freer to experiment. Old groundless fears were proven to be just that—groundless . . . As for basketball, the best was yet to come."

Chapter 8

Integration of the NBA

I n 1946, World War II was over and Americans were ready to enjoy an era of peace, prosperity, and the freedom to pursue happiness. That year the United Nations General Assembly held its first session, British Prime Minister Winston Churchill made his famous "Iron Curtain" speech in Fulton, Missouri, warning the world about Communism, and Ethel Merman starred in the hit Broadway musical *Annie Get Your Gun.*

In 1946, however, racial tensions were drawn to the snapping point. Black soldiers returning from the war wanted their share of the democratic pie. They were no longer willing to accept second-class citizenship in a nation they had helped to defend. In response to black demands for equality and justice, race riots errupted in Columbia, Tennessee, in February and in Athens, Georgia, in August. Blacks were murdered and their houses and businesses burned. Further infuriating segregationists, Brooklyn Dodgers general manager Branch Rickey had surprised America in 1945 by signing Jackie

Robinson, the first African American to play major-league baseball since the 1890s. During 1946 Robinson was playing with the Dodgers' leading farm club, the Montreal Royals, in the International League.

Robinson, who had been a star athlete at UCLA, was selected not just for his ability to play baseball, but also because Rickey believed Robinson had the temperament, the character, and commitment to endure the pressure of being the "first." Being the first to do anything is difficult, but being the first African American to break into the major leagues carried an extra burden. From the day he took to the field, Jackie Robinson was subjected to all kinds of abuse, ranging from hate mail to death threats and from fans calling him names to players trying to hurt his legs by sliding into second base, his position, with their cleats up around his shins. Even some of his own teammates refused to accept him simply because he was black.

Robinson's every action and reaction was scrutinized in the press. If he lost his temper or buckled under the pressure it would have been a setback to the integration of baseball. All his critics wanted was for him to fail, so they could block other blacks from entering the majors.

On January 3, 1947, the NAACP issued a report that said 1946 was "one of the grimmest years in the history" of the organization. Black veterans had been hanged, shot, even blowtorched; some had their eyes gouged out. "Negroes in America have been disillusioned over

William "Pop" Gates lasted only one season on the previously all-white Tri-Cities Blackhawks because of an on-court scuffle with a white player from an opposing team. [Naismith Memorial Basketball Hall of Fame]

the wave of lynchings, brutality and official recession from all of the flamboyant promises of post-war democracy and decency," the report continued.

In a climate of racial hostility, Jackie Robinson opened the 1947 baseball season with the Brooklyn Dodgers. His success paved the way for other black baseball players such as Larry Doby, who joined the Cleveland Indians in July, and Dan Bankhead, Willard Brown, and Henry Thompson, who also joined the majors in 1947.

While black baseball players were making baseball history, Rens stars Pop Gates and William "Dolly" King were going unnoticed playing hoops with the Tri-

Cities Blackhawks of the previously all-white Basketball Association of America (BAA). But not all athletes
were willing to turn the other cheek when players and
fans committed atrocities against them. Gates said that
he and King lasted only one season because of an on-
court fight between Chick Meehan of the Syracuse
Nationals and himself.

"Meehan . . . threw me down one time, and I said,
'Chick, don't do that no more!' " Gates said, remem-
bering the incident. "Well, he threw me once again. So,
I deliberately placed myself in the pivot. When he tried
again, I threw him down and he got up whaling. So I
got mine [punch] in first before he got his in. I made
him bleed. That's the reason Dolly and I only played
one season."

By today's standards the on-court scuffle between
Gates and Meehan would be considered minor and
maybe draw a technical foul or perhaps a game sus-
pension. But in 1946, if a black man threw a punch at
a white man for any reason, he could be jailed or in
some states lynched.

Life for Gates and King during that year, even
though they played on teams with white ballplayers,
was very difficult. They couldn't sleep in the same hotel
and they often had to spend the night in private homes
or at a "colored" YMCA. The situation, however, was
very different for the Globetrotters club.

The Globetrotters finished the 1947–48 season with

a 52-game winning streak, a victory in the Cuba Invitational basketball tournament, a win over the Minneapolis Lakers, and contracts for two movies, *The Globetrotters* and *Go, Man, Go.*

During this time, the 'Trotters were playing big and living large, because many BAA owners became more interested in filling arenas than heeding racial barriers. Even though some owners agreed not to sign black players, they quickly booked games against the Globetrotters, because they always outdrew regular season games.

Unfortunately, the Rens played their final game on March 21, 1949. Meanwhile members of the better-known Eastern BAA merged with the Midwest-centered National Basketball Association (NBA). Writer Nelson George notes that if the Rens had held on for just one more season they would have been given an automatic berth in the fledgling NBA. Having a black-owned professional basketball team in the NBA at the start could have had a significant impact on sports history for generations.

Even though, by 1950, President Harry S Truman had integrated the United States military, segregation in mainstream American schools, neighborhoods, and corporations remained the norm. The desegregation of sports, however, continued in spite of the slow progress being made in education, housing, and employment.

93

Then, on April 25, 1950, the NBA teams named the players that they wanted to sign up, a process called the "draft." Walter Brown, founder of the Boston Celtics, announced in the second round of draft picks: "Boston takes Charles Cooper of Duquesne." You could have heard a pin drop during the closed-door session at a Chicago hotel.

According to *The New York Times* columnist George

Walter Brown, founder of the Boston Celtics, made history in 1950 during the second round of NBA draft picks with six words: "Boston takes Charles Cooper of Duquesne." [AP/Wide World]

Sullivan, an owner from another club spoke up. "Walter, don't you know he's a colored boy?" To which Brown replied, "I don't [care] if he's striped, plaid, or polka-dot! Boston takes Charles Cooper of Duquesne."

It was as simple as that.

Cooper was an all-American forward who had experienced his fair share of racism on and off the court. Although Duquesne was scheduled to play Tennessee, the Volunteers refused to play an integrated team. Officials at Duquesne wouldn't give in, and Tennessee went home. "It didn't cause me any kind of emotional anguish," recalled Cooper. "If that was what they wanted to do, let them go back to Tennessee. As long as nobody called me a 'nigger' it was all right. 'Nigger' automatically meant a fight!"

Cooper said that he wasn't surprised at being drafted by the Celtics. A scout, Art Spector, had discussed the possibility. When Walter Brown made his historic announcement, Cooper was on a three-week tour with the Globetrotters. In the ninth round of the same draft, the Washington Capitols picked Earl Lloyd of West Virginia State. Also that season, Nat "Sweetwater" Clifton had his contract purchased from the Globetrotters by the New York Knicks.

It was finally done. White owners in the NBA had drafted two black players and bought the services of another. This wasn't due to any magnanimity of the owners; they knew that good black players would help them win games. Winners filled seats. And seats translated into revenue.

The 1950 draft marked the end of Abe Saperstein's dominance of black basketball players. Saperstein was furious. "Abe went crazy," Wilt Chamberlain said. "He threatened to boycott the Boston Garden." According to Nelson George, "Given the opportunity to play fewer games for more money with no clowning required, the best black players started to ignore Saperstein's blandishments against the NBA."

Earl Lloyd was the first of the three black 1950 NBA draft picks to compete. On October 31, 1950, Lloyd took the court against Rochester in an away game. The Washington team folded in January 1951 with a dismal record of 10–25, and the big 6-foot 5-inch, 220-pound forward was then drafted into the army. Lloyd returned during the 1952–53 season to play with the Syracuse Nationals. He played there for six years and then two more for Detroit, before he retired in 1960.

"[Lloyd] was always doing the dirty work, fouling out of the game," says Dolph Shayes, a teammate from Syracuse. "Actually, he helped me a great deal because with him in there I was free to rebound and get a lot of glory, since his game was to guard the other team's offensive ace."

Charles Cooper played both forward and guard for the Celtics for four seasons. During his rookie season he grabbed 562 rebounds, dished 174 assists, and averaged

9.3 points per game. Still, racism and discrimination hounded him wherever he played. "Traveling around the league, I encountered all the problems of any black man of that period—be he a diplomat, a porter, or a basketball player," said Cooper during an interview. The story was a familiar one. He had to sleep in different hotels than his white teammates. "My teammates and the management acquiesced to this like everybody else at the time," Cooper continued. "Only later when things had changed somewhat and players with stature like Bill Russell and Elgin Baylor came along did conditions get better. Being superstars and working in a better environment, they could boycott games if they felt things were unfair." Cooper also said that he didn't feel like a pioneer. He gave full credit to Jackie Robinson, saying "he's the one who shouldered the burden that helped blacks in other sports. He was the pioneer."

The third black player who joined the NBA in 1950 was Nat "Sweetwater" Clifton, who left the Globetrotters to sign with the Knicks. Clifton, who had played college basketball at Xavier College in New Orleans, was one of the flashier members of the Globetrotters. In the summer of 1950, Clifton found out that the white all-star team the 'Trotters were playing against made more money. He told his teammates, and Saperstein regarded this as treason.

Saperstein knew the Knicks were interested in having

a black player, so he sold Clifton's contract to them. Saperstein said he sold it for $5,000 and gave Clifton half. Later, Clifton learned that the contract was sold for $20,000, but it was not a time for looking back.

Clifton spent seven seasons with the Knicks, averaging 10.3 points per game. He was never able to fully change from the flash-and-dash style of the Globetrotters to the slower, more inhibited style of the Knicks. "I would have been happy playing with the Knicks," said Clifton in an interview, "but the thing is, all the time I played there, they never did get another good black ballplayer to play with me—somebody who knew what I was doing, you understand? That kinda held me back, 'cause you can't do something with the other guys because they played the straight way."

In 1958, Clifton moved to the Detroit Pistons, where he teamed up with another black player, Walter Dukes. There is an often-told story about the duo. While playing against St. Louis, the 7-foot Dukes got in a fight with fans after a name-calling incident. Referee Norm Drucker said he saw Clifton running to assist Dukes. Clifton yelled, "Walter, you take the first row, I've got the second row." Fans soon learned that basketball players were not going to accept the verbal or physical abuse that fans had heaped on Jackie Robinson. The harassment began to abate. Perhaps times were changing and people were becoming more accepting.

One of Chuck Cooper's teammates, Bob Cousy (left), was the first white player to adopt the playing style of black ballplayers. [UPI/Corbis-Bettmann]

Clifton went on to play four seasons with the Harlem Magicians, reuniting with former Globetrotter teammates Marques Haynes and Goose Tatum. Ironically, Clifton finished his career playing for Saperstein and the Globetrotters. A knee injury ended his playing days in 1965.

Clifton and Cooper were known for their fast-paced, showy style of playing. They were derided by basketball pundits as "showboat performers" rather than good players. The first white player to adopt the style of black ballplayers was Bob Cousy, a skinny kid from Queens who was a star at Holy Cross College in Massachusetts. Cousy and Cooper were teammates on the Celtics. "Cousy is about as free from the affliction of racism as any white person I've ever known," said Cooper.

Cousy's behind-the-back dribble, no-glance passes, and long shots made him popular with the fans and sportswriters. But these were the same moves that sportswriters, coaches, and fans criticized Clifton and Cooper for. Eventually, respect for both styles of play developed.

Although there may be disagreement about the importance of their role in the development of basketball, it surely took a lot of courage for Cooper, Clifton, and Lloyd to be the first blacks to play in the NBA. They paved the way for other black athletes to be sports pioneers. Althea Gibson and Arthur Ashe in tennis, Grant Fuhr in hockey, and Pélé in soccer all stood on the shoulders of these early athletes and made it possible for athletes of all colors to participate in sports at all levels.

Chapter 9

The David and Goliath of the NCAA

The 1960s will be remembered for many culture-shaking events. The civil rights movement was in full swing, the Vietnam War, the cold war, the yippies, Woodstock, the assassinations of John and Robert Kennedy, Malcolm X, and Martin Luther King, Jr., and humans landing on the moon by the end of the decade were just some of the events that would help mold America in the last decades of the twentieth century.

Few people would list the victory of five young black men from a small college in El Paso, Texas, over a team from a large all-white university in Lexington, Kentucky, with some of these better-known events of the 1960s. But, at least in the annals of college basketball, Hall of Fame coach Don Hoskins's Texas Western's 71–65 whipping of an all-star-studded University of Kentucky squad to win the 1966 NCAA tournament is still a big deal.

Adolph Rupp, also a Hall of Fame coach, had refused to recruit blacks. And why should he? First, his Kentucky Wildcats were doing fine without black players. Second, why put up with the wrath of racists and recruit an African-American player?

Texas Western's 1966 victory was not an aberration; black players had become more and more important on college and professional basketball teams. The victory also didn't occur by happenstance; other schools around the country had come close to winning national titles with four black starters.

In 1963, for example, Chicago's Loyola University had played with as many as four blacks on the court throughout the season. During the first round of the NCAA tournament, George Ireland's Ramblers handily beat two all-white Southern teams, Tennessee Tech and Mississippi State, on their way to the finals against the University of Cincinnati Bearcats. The Bearcats were also a well-integrated team that was expected to win a third straight title, but the national television audience saw the Loyola Ramblers win a close one, 60–58. Black players contributed to the efforts of both teams.

Another significant event in the 1963 tournament was the fact that the Mississippi State Bulldogs showed up at all. They were almost denied a chance to play by school officials, who had passed up invitations in the past because of the possibility of the races mixing on the court.

A state court had approved an injunction to keep the team from participating in "race mixing," but not before the Bulldogs had made it out of the state and to

Texas Western's five black starting players surprised the all-white, star-studded University of Kentucky squad by whipping them soundly to win the 1966 NCAA tournament. [UPI/Corbis-Bettmann]

the tournament site. Babe McCarthy, coach of the Bulldogs, believed that his team had a right to play against the best schools in the country, so he took the chance and defied the injunction. Although McCarthy's boys lost that night to Loyola, 61–51, his actions were about as brave as any coach's in that decade.

Texas Western's starting five went 23–1 during the 1965–66 season, but the team was often criticized for playing a free-wheeling offense that featured fancy passing, dribbling, fast breaks, and lots of shots. When compared to the white teams of that time, teams that played a slowed-down, high-percentage-shot game, Texas Western looked "undisciplined."

"[Texas Western was] a step or two swifter than most opponents, and over the course of a game that difference, plus intensity, resulted in easy lay-ups and created turnovers," Nelson George wrote. "Blinded by bigotry, many claimed the Miners . . . didn't play intelligently."

One wonders, if the "free-wheeling" team had been all-white, would those players have been said to be aggressive and improvisational?

The Miners' opponents were the more traditional Kentucky Wildcats, with their storied and well-heeled coach, Adolph Rupp, who had gone out of his way not to play teams with black players. When Rupp did play them, the results were sometimes embarrassing. In New York in 1950, Rupp suffered one of his more humiliating defeats at the hands of an integrated City College of New York team, 89–50.

What most critics of the Miners failed to point out or completely ignored were the similarities between Texas Western and Kentucky. Both teams relied on quickness and passing. And despite protestations to the contrary, both teams were disciplined and well-coached.

As good as the Wildcats were, the Miners were just a little faster, a little bit more aggressive, and certainly more innovative. The Miners' tight defense led to scoring on fast breaks, and the team hit their free throws down the stretch to beat Kentucky.

Unfortunately, it was discovered that the five starters were not good students. Indeed, a couple were flunking out. Hoskins was accused of exploitation, and the ordeal took some of the luster off the victory. "Over time many of the Texas Western starters did earn their degrees, but their athletic pimping revealed the dark side of Black players and white school education," Nelson George wrote.

This was the beginning of what has plagued the relationship between white universities and black athletes. It was one thing to open the gym and locker room to black athletes; it was quite another to open the entire university. Their court appearances were for their athletic ability, which in turn made alumni happy. Happy alumni meant money.

In the 1980s, some called for stricter entrance requirements for college athletes, such as minimum SAT or ACT scores, high school grade-point average of at least 2.0, and a certain number of college prep courses. Georgetown coach John Thompson shouted that this was racism, but it fell on deaf ears. In order to ask for such things from inner-city athletes, chronically underfunded schools would have to be overhauled at a time when school budgets were being slashed.

To Arthur Ashe, this was a vicious circle. "As the

rewards of a professional basketball career increased, so did the temptation to push through the nation's public-school systems those athletically gifted but academically unprepared players. Many blacks graduated from high school with elementary reading-skill levels. The overwhelming majority of black professional players were from families in lower socioeconomic groups. As such, they were more inclined to spend the thousands of hours of practice necessary to make their high school and college teams."

It's not known how much time Kareem Abdul-Jabbar spent in the schoolyard, but he shows how black athletes could balance athletics and education.

Abdul-Jabbar was born Lewis Alcindor on April 16, 1947, in New York City. He is the son of Caribbean natives who immigrated to the United States. Alcindor changed his name to Kareem Abdul-Jabbar in 1971 when he converted to the Muslim religion.

Alcindor was a standout at the Catholic school Power Memorial High in New York City. He scored a record 2,067 points, grabbed 2,002 rebounds, and led his team to 71 straight victories while at Power Memorial.

Alcindor was also a standout academically, making him a prized recruit for many universities around the country. Alcindor moved to California to play for the UCLA Bruins. In 1966, he led the freshman squad to an undefeated season. From 1967 through 1969, he led

Kareem Abdul-Jabbar (formerly Lew Alcindor) showed that basketball players could achieve a good balance of academics and athletics. [AP/Wide World]

UCLA to three national championships and was named the top player of the tournament each of those years.

Alcindor's choice to play for UCLA and its legendary coach, John Wooden, was interesting. Wooden was born in basketball-crazy Indiana and starred at Purdue University. While Indiana had an ugly reputation as a racist state, Wooden himself did not tolerate bigotry. Indeed, Wooden's belief that African Americans should not be excluded from the opportunity to play big-time Division I basketball, and to attend a well-respected university, is what attracted many black players to UCLA.

The Bruins, and their crosstown rival University of Southern California, had a reputation as progressive institutions. UCLA was home to many black student-athletes, including Jackie Robinson and Nobel laureate Ralph Bunche.

This is not to say that all was well all the time. Wooden demanded discipline and adherence to a team approach to basketball. There was no room for show-offs, hot dogs, or flashy moves.

Walt Hazzard, a point guard who in 1964 helped guide the Bruins to the first of their five titles in six seasons, was benched early in his UCLA career because Wooden thought he was too flashy. What Hazzard was doing in the early '60s is something that most point guards do now—dribbling the ball between his legs and making passes from behind his

The moves that got Walt Hazzard benched for being "too flashy" in the '60s are performed by most of today's point guards. [UPI/Corbis-Bettmann]

back. Hazzard thought his coach's complaints were unreasonable. The moves were fooling defenders and the passes were hitting the mark. Wooden's complaints were based on his view that Hazzard was doing something undisciplined and unorthodox rather than inventive and talented.

Instead of Hazzard changing his style, Coach Wooden built an offense around his guard's skills. Wooden centered everything from the high post and relied on Hazzard's and the team's quickness to set picks and run intricate patterns.

All of this led the Bruins to a perfect 33–0 season.

When the 7-foot 2-inch Alcindor entered UCLA, he immediately posed a problem with a style different from that of Wooden's previous teams. Most of Wooden's squads featured players no taller than 6 feet 5 inches; Hazzard was a tall point guard at 6 feet 2 inches. Wooden's challenge was how to make use of a tall, mobile center in the low post in an offense keyed to the guards on the high posts.

Once again, Coach Wooden changed his style in order to make use of his best player. Most tall men did not have the speed and agility Alcindor possessed. "I wanted [Alcindor] no further from the offensive basket than he could reach . . . no more than eight feet away," Wooden said.

On the defensive end, Wooden let Alcindor cover the baseline, allowing UCLA's forwards, who would normally be tied up deep in the low post, to be more aggressive.

How successful was this retooled offense? The Bruins won three championships from 1967 to 1969 and amassed a record of 88–3, with Alcindor leading the way. His offensive numbers were incredible, averaging 26.4 points per game with a shooting percentage of 62.4. It should also be noted that Alcindor did well in the classroom too, graduating with his class.

Lew Alcindor was drafted by the Milwaukee Bucks, an expansion club, in 1969. He signed a five-year,

$1.2 million contract and was worth every penny. He was second in the league in scoring in his rookie season, averaging 28.8 points per game, and grabbed 1,190 boards. Alcindor was named the NBA's Rookie of the Year and was on the second-team all-NBA squad.

In 1971, he teamed with Oscar Robertson, and the two led the Bucks to the franchise's only NBA title. He was named the NBA's Most Valuable Player and first-team all-NBA, averaging 31.7 points and just over 16 rebounds per game.

Despite leading the Bucks to four straight playoff appearances, Jabbar wanted out of Milwaukee and was traded to the Los Angeles Lakers in 1975, where his legend would grow even larger.

By the time he retired in 1989, Kareem Abdul-Jabbar had played in 1,560 games, logging 57,446 minutes in the NBA, and had scored 38,387 points. He led the Lakers to five titles, was named the league's Most Valuable Player six times, and was named to the all-NBA team 10 times.

His unstoppable move was the sky hook, where he would jump-hook the ball over everyone and hit the basket. But he also blocked shots and was known as one of the best defensive centers in the game.

Chapter 10

Dr. J, Magic, Bird, Jordan, and Shaq

The 1970s in basketball were defined by a period of ambivalence among the sport's fans. Basketball was an obsession in the inner city, where all you needed was a hoop and a basketball or even a soccer ball.

But among the rest of America, basketball was third, behind baseball and football. There were two theories as to why. First, many whites did not want to watch a game that was dominated by black players, especially players who not only rejected the notion that they were subservient to white coaches, owners, and fans but also rejected what some thought were "normal" American ideals. Kareem Abdul-Jabbar, for example, was one of several black athletes who joined the Muslim faith. Bobby Moore, a football player for the St. Louis Cardinals, changed his name to Ahmad Reeshad and was soundly booed by the home crowd and by people across the country. Some shortsightedly saw this as being anti-American.

The second theory was that the media hyped stereotypes of black players as undisciplined, abrasive, ungrateful, and spoiled. Arthur Ashe lamented the way in which some Americans viewed a professional sport that was increasingly being dominated by black men. "Ted Stepien, the Cleveland Cavaliers owner, said he thought attendance would rise if there were more white players," Ashe wrote. "In New York City, the Knicks were sometimes referred to by some whites as the New York Niggerbockers."

On the opposite end was the idea that black players, because they were well paid, were somehow proof that racism no longer existed. In fact, the idea that a sport could survive because it was dominated by blacks showed the racial divide in the country.

The American Basketball Association (ABA), which formed in 1966 as an alternative league to the NBA, also had problems with racism. In the 1970s, the Dallas ABA team had to drop 4 of their 10 black players because, as a team official said, "Whites in Dallas are simply not interested in paying to see an all-black team, and the black population alone cannot support us."

The sportswriters of the day theorized that somehow the product was inferior and that was what was keeping whites away from the game. In fact, the field goal percentage in the 1970s was .527, compared to .432 in 1951.

That the game was getting better and better could be

Many later hoop stars, like Michael Jordan, modeled themselves after Julius "Dr. J" Erving. [UPI/Corbis-Bettmann]

seen in the graceful moves and artistry of Julius "Dr. J" Erving, who played for the Virginia Squires and New Jersey Nets of the ABA and later with the Philadelphia 76ers in the NBA. Erving is the player whom later hoop stars such as Michael Jordan, Penny Hardaway, Grant Hill, and others modeled themselves after.

Julius W. Erving II was born on February 22, 1950, in Roosevelt, New York. He starred at the University of Massachusetts, where he averaged 26.9 points per game in 1971. He also grabbed 527 boards. Not bad for a guard.

Erving left Massachusetts early, not because of a big bonus or because he was flunking out of school, but because he wanted to help pay some of his mother's hospital bills. He was invited to the Virginia Squires training camp and immediately caught everyone's attention by leaping over five guys for a dunk.

What Erving excelled at in professional basketball was being able to almost fly to the hoop. Sometimes on a breakaway, and in full stride, he would take off from the free-throw line and glide up to the basket, palming the ball with one hand and jamming it into the net. He made it look effortless. "A young Julius Erving was like a Thomas Edison," said Johnny Kerr, an announcer for the Squires at the time. "He was inventing something new every night."

Erving would become a member of two ABA championship teams and was named the Most Valuable Player three times before the ABA merged with the NBA in 1976.

Erving's deft moves on the court, his gravity-defying dunks, and his commanding presence on and off the court are what people remember about him since his retirement in 1987. He averaged 22 points per game in 11 seasons in the NBA and 21.9 per game during the playoffs. Erving was named the NBA's Most Valuable Player in 1977 and the MVP of the All-Star Game in 1985.

Despite such players as Erving, Walt Frazier, Kareem

Abdul-Jabbar, Oscar Robertson, Elvin Hayes, and Earl "The Pearl" Monroe, professional basketball was still not packing in the crowds that owners and league officials thought it could. This all turned around when two young men—one black, the other white—entered the NBA in 1979.

Earvin "Magic" Johnson and Larry Bird played in one of the most exciting NCAA tournaments in history. Johnson's Michigan State Spartans defeated Larry Bird and Indiana State in the 1979 championship game.

Magic Johnson (center) and Larry Bird (left) were two of the star players who ushered in the Golden Era of Basketball. [AP/Wide World]

Larry Bird went off and starred for the Boston Celtics, where he was considered—whether he wanted to be or not—the Great White Hope of basketball. That was unfortunate, because Bird was more interested in becoming one of the greatest hoopsters of all time than in being important because of the racial implications of his presence.

What made Bird so impressive was that though he lacked the foot speed of many other players, he had, just like Magic Johnson and other great players, a keen sense of what was going on around him. His peripheral vision must have been incredible, because he was known for making wickedly fast and deadly accurate passes without much of an effort. He was also deft at hitting the three-point shot, and he could penetrate and drive the lane, and hit from deep in the low post.

Bird and Magic Johnson, who was born on August 14, 1959, in Lansing, Michigan, were just what the league needed: a spark. The combination of Johnson and Jabbar with the Los Angeles Lakers in the 1979–80 season was the beginning of a Golden Era in Basketball.

Johnson's moves on the court were ingenious, considering his 6-foot 9-inch height. Remember, UCLA had won championships in the early 1960s with no player taller than 6 feet 5 inches, but here were the Lakers 15 years later showcasing a fast, powerful, intelligent guard who could easily have played as a forward or a small center.

Small center? Yes. As a matter of fact, one of Johnson's most memorable performances was against the Philadelphia 76ers in the 1980 NBA title game. The Erving-led 76ers (with Darryl Dawkins, a center with a dunk so awesome that he shattered a number of back-boards and was nicknamed "Chocolate Thunder") were down 3–2 in a best-of-seven series. An injury to Jabbar, who'd averaged 24 points per game that season, made it look as if the 76ers might be able to shift the momentum to their side for game six. It was not to be.

Paul Westhead, the Lakers' coach, decided to start Johnson at center against Dawkins and Caldwell Jones, another tall, aggressive center. Magic's leaping ability, agility, and speed proved too much for the bigger and stronger 76er duo. Magic ended the game with 42 points, 15 rebounds, and 7 assists while playing an unfamiliar position. Magic Johnson began to be spoken of in the same breath with other basketball greats.

"Where [Bill] Russell [of the Boston Celtics] reinvented basketball defense, Magic Johnson destroyed all stereotypical notions of how size dictated positions and, along with Bird, glorified creative passing and teamwork," Nelson George wrote.

Although people tried to draw a distinction between the styles of play of Magic and Bird—the flashy Laker vs. the blue-collar Celtic—both were the personification of what basketball was supposed to be when Naismith invented it: a game where teamwork *and* individual excellence matter. Both players were above-average scorers, but excellent passers as well. Their physical and mental attributes inspired their teams.

"The player I admired most was Magic Johnson," Bird said. "I've never seen anybody as good as him." Johnson won five NBA titles in 13 seasons with the Lakers. He was named the league's MVP for the play-offs in 1980 (the first rookie ever to be given such an award), 1982, and 1987. He was the league's MVP in 1987, 1989, and 1990, and the MVP of the All-Star Game in 1990 and 1992. He also won a gold medal for the United States during the 1992 Olympics.

It is his 1992 all-star MVP that is especially memorable. Magic had retired in November 1991, after it was discovered that he was HIV positive. "This is not like my life is over," Johnson said after his retirement. "I plan on going on living for a long time. This is just another challenge."

But the disease, which was brought to the forefront of national discussion with Johnson's announcement, had cut short a career much too early, just as it has done with many other men and women.

Magic tried to come back twice, retiring not too long after starting again. For a time during the 1993 season he coached the Lakers. In his career, Johnson scored over 17,000 points—19.7 points per game. He also accumulated 136 triple-doubles in points, rebounds, and assists.

Another highlight for Magic was finally teaming up with Bird, as well as with Michael Jordan, Scottie Pippen, Patrick Ewing, and other NBA stars, in the 1992 Olympic Games in Barcelona. The Dream Team went undefeated, winning handily and taking home America's second gold medal in basketball since 1968. (Jordan led the team in 1984, but was repeatedly told that it didn't count for much because the Russians didn't play.)

Magic Johnson thanks his father for making him the basketball player he was. "He instilled unselfishness into me and all my brothers and sisters," Johnson said. "And if you didn't get the message, he would take you over the knee and explain what he was trying to say. He made me learn the game from both sides—scoring and also passing. He's the big reason why I became the player I was."

If Magic Johnson and Larry Bird, along with a host of others, opened the gates to a new approach to basketball, then it was Michael Jordan who picked up on it. Jordan has developed into everything good in basketball. He was talented on and off the ball, on defense and offense, and on and off the court. His endorsements have netted him $30 million a year.

Jordan takes off on dunks the way Dr. J did. His defense is as tenacious as Bill Russell's. He can control the game the way Johnson did. He lifts his teammates the way both Johnson and Bird did. And he works as hard in practice as he does in a game.

Though Michael Jordan did not make the cut the first time he tried out for his high school basketball team, he became what many consider to be the best basketball player of all time. [AP/Wide World/Chuck Stoody]

"I feel like I have a reputation to defend," Jordan said about his intensity. "I want them to know what they might have heard isn't gossip or rumors. I want them to know it all comes from hard work. I want them to know I deserve what I get. And it all starts in practice."

Michael Jordan, a North Carolinian, and Bill Russell started off the same way, inasmuch as both did not make their high school teams. But Jordan was able to turn his game around and make it to the University of North Carolina, one of the most prestigious schools in the country. Playing for the Tar Heels, especially if you are from North Carolina, is akin to being from Montreal and playing for the Canadiens or being from the Bronx and playing for the Yankees. His exploits at North Carolina are legendary, but that almost goes without saying for a guy who scored the winning basket in the 1982 NCAA championship—as a freshman.

"I've seen some great athletes, but Michael also has the intelligence, the court savvy . . . he was a hero so many times at the end of the game—it was uncanny," North Carolina coach Dean Smith told *Inside Sports* in 1985.

Jordan's early career was tough. He was a high-scoring star on a perennially losing team, the Chicago Bulls. Finally he was able to break through with his first championship ring in 1991, with teammates Scottie Pippen and Horace Grant. He won two more rings before the murder of his father and the constant media attention made him give up the game for 17 months. During that time, he played minor-league baseball for the Birmingham Barons in the class AA Southern League.

Jordan returned to the game in the winter of 1995, and most people didn't give him a shot at being as good as he was when he left the game, much less at leading his team back to the finals. Imagine everyone's surprise when he scored 55 points on the road against the Knicks, shortly after returning to basketball. The Bulls won titles in 1996 and 1997, averaging more than 70 wins in each season. By 1997 Jordan had won eight NBA scoring titles, four MVP awards, one Defensive Player of the Year award, four NBA Finals MVP awards, two All-Star Game MVPs, and two slam dunk titles, and had led the NBA three times in steals.

Nelson George may have summed up Jordan best when he wrote: "Even among the all-time greats Jordan has few peers: He hangs as long and high as Elgin Baylor and Julius Erving, he combines rebounding and passing like Oscar Robertson but is quicker and more deceptive, and his will is as steely as Russell's or anyone else who has laced up sneakers."

The person most likely to take Jordan's basketball mantle is a 7-foot 1-inch, 300-pound giant named Shaquille O'Neal—if he gets better at free-throw shooting. But when it comes to playing his position, O'Neal has few peers. He's already being compared to Wilt Chamberlain, a comparison Shaq's taken a liking to.

"I'm sort of like Wilt Chamberlain, a scorer, real strong, dominant," O'Neal said. "If I can get the dunk ten times out of ten, I'm going for the dunk ten times out of ten."

O'Neal, who also credits his father for helping him develop as a ballplayer and as a man, was a two-time all-American at Louisiana State University before being drafted after his junior year by the Orlando Magic in 1992. He wasted no time in making his mark. O'Neal was selected the NBA's Player of the Week the first week of his rookie season in 1993, was the first rookie

Shaquille O'Neal shooting over Seattle's Jim McIlvaine during a playoff game. [AP/Wide World]

to start on the NBA All-Star team since Michael Jordan, and was named that season's Rookie of the Year.

In his second season he led the league in shooting percentage and the following year he was the scoring champion, while leading the Magic to the NBA Finals in 1994.

In August 1996, the Los Angeles Lakers signed the twenty-four-year-old O'Neal to a contract worth $120 million. Like so many stars before him, O'Neal wants to be the best at what he does.

"He is a dedicated basketball player," says Laker coach Del Harris. "He wants to improve and he wants to win games, yet he's got such a light-hearted spirit, he can break up a pressured situation."

Chapter 11

Black Women in Basketball

T he history of women's basketball can be traced to Senda Berenson, a teacher at Smith College in Massachusetts, who adopted Naismith's rules in 1896 to suit the young women she taught. Berenson was a graduate of Boston Normal School of Gymnastics, a school known for being open-minded and liberal. If only Berenson, the mother of women's basketball in the United States, could see what the game is like a hundred years later: the "Dream Team" in American women's basketball has won an Olympic gold medal; two solid professional basketball leagues have been formed—the Women's National Basketball Association and the American Basketball League; and a collegiate women's basketball tournament attracts thousands of fans to the Final Four and hundreds of thousands more on television.

At Smith, a highly selective women's college, Berenson's need to find new ways of keeping up the enthusiasm of her students was almost akin to Naismith's need five years earlier. Berenson's changes,

The first women's basketball team was formed at Smith College. Players wore uniforms of black bloomers and long stockings, and men were not allowed to attend their games. [Smith College Archives]

however, made the women's game less fast-paced than the men's game. She split the court into three zones, with two players from each team in each zone. (The two-court game for women wasn't adopted until 1938, and the women's game featured six-on-six until the 1971–72 season.) The players could not move out of their zones, and guarding, passing, and dribbling were severely limited. And unlike today's players, who wear shorts and T-shirts for uniforms, the women of Smith wore bloomers and long black stockings on the court.

Despite what we would consider hindrances, Berenson's students were wholly enthusiastic about their first game, which featured two teams made up of women from the college. The final score isn't known, and men were not allowed to attend the game.

The game spread quickly throughout the United States. Vassar and Wellesley women began playing in 1896 and 1898 respectively, and the first intercollegiate game between women took place in 1898 in Berkeley, California, between the University of California and Stanford University, a school that would play a major role in women's basketball in the 1980s and 1990s. The game, also played without men present, attracted several hundred cheering fans, mostly from Cal.

According to the *Women's Encyclopedia of Sports*, women's basketball almost didn't survive past the late 1890s. "Competitiveness, stoutly discouraged, was thought to be harmful to tender female psyches, and matches had already been marred by hair-pulling incidents. Nevertheless basketball survived, with influential defenders inside and outside the system." One of those defenders from the outside was Phoebe Hearts, whose 1901 gift to the University of California was an outdoor basketball court.

Women's basketball even made it to the Olympics in 1922 and 1928, but was then discontinued until 1976. After a fast start, women's basketball drifted on the intercollegiate level. A national tournament sponsored by the Association of Intercollegiate Athletics for Women (AIAW) was adopted in 1972. The National

It was considered "out of the question" for the first black women's basketball teams to perform in short pants or for money. [Schomburg Center for Research in Black Culture, New York Public Library]

Collegiate Athletic Association (NCAA) took over the national collegiate tournament in 1982. It draws more and more fans each season to its March Madness and Final Four games, both in person and watching on TV.

The record on the early years of black women and basketball is sketchy. Some men's teams from the early 1900s fielded teams for women. The Smart Set, a club team from Brooklyn, and Wissahickon from Philadelphia, were two of the more well-known black women's teams. "Dore Cole and her sisters dominated the first Smart Set team and soon had imitators who played their games in blousy knee-length bloomers and long-sleeved shirts," according to Arthur Ashe in *A Hard Road to Glory*. "The idea of performing in short pants—or for money—was simply out of the question for women."

The two best teams in the early history of black women's basketball were the Chicago Romas and the *Philadelphia Tribune* squad. The Romas, organized by Edward "Sol" Butler, featured Isadore Channels, a four-time winner of the American Tennis Association (ATA) women's singles title. Other Romas players included Corinne Robinson, Mignon Burns, Lillian Ross, Virginia Willis, and Lula Porter. The Romas were the dominant team in Chicago and throughout the Midwest. The *Philadelphia Tribune* squad, sponsored by the black weekly bearing its name, started operations in 1931. Like other women's teams, they played a six-on-six game but they also, from time to time, played five-on-five full-court basketball like the men. In either realm, they were tops.

The *Tribune* squad was led by Ora Washington, who (like Channels of the Romas) was a tennis star as well. Washington, a basketball center, won eight ATA singles titles. Her basketball teammates included Gladys Walker, Virginia Woods, Lavinia Moore, Myrtle Wilson, Rose Wilson, Marie Leach, Florence Campbell, and Sarah Latimere. They were credited by most black newspapers with being the unofficial national champions through the 1930s, and by the time they disbanded in 1940, the *Philadelphia Tribune* squad's fame among black female athletes almost equaled that of the Tuskegee women's track team that won the Amateur Athletic Union championship.

Black school teams, in an era when records were better kept, ranked among the top teams in women's basketball during the 1970s and 1980s. South Carolina State University, for example, won the AIAW II national championship in 1979. Virginia Union and Hampton University won NCAA Division II titles in 1983 and 1988 respectively.

Probably the best-known black women's coach of the era is Vivian Stringer, who raked up a record of 251–51 at Pennsylvania's Cheney State from 1971 to 1982. At Cheney, Stringer got the school to the finals of the first NCAA women's championship, eventually losing to Louisiana Tech. Stringer was named head coach of the

Iowa Hawkeyes, a sorry program that she raised to become one of the top in the country. Stringer, in fact, became the first woman to lead two separate schools to a national ranking of number two or better. In 1995 Rutgers, another struggling program, paid her $150,000 per year to lead the Scarlet Knights to victory.

The International Olympic Committee reinstated women's basketball as an official medal sport for the 1976 games in Montreal. The United States defeated Bulgaria 95–79 to win the silver medal behind the Soviet Union. It would be eight years before the women would have a chance to show their skills again on the international stage; the United States boycotted the 1980 Games in Moscow because of the Soviet Union's invasion of Afghanistan.

In 1984, the United States had its first Dream Team, with Cheryl Miller and Lynette Woodard on the court and Pat Head Summitt coaching. The United States defeated Korea to win the gold medal—the first for a U.S. women's basketball team—at an Olympics marred by the absence of the Soviet team, which boycotted the 1984 Los Angeles Games.

Miller, a 6-foot 3-inch forward, was nicknamed "Silk" for a reason. While playing high school ball in Riverside, California, she once scored 105 points—in one game. She is also the first woman to dunk in organized competition. While at the University of Southern California, Miller was named to the all-American team

Cheryl Miller (number 31) was the first woman to dunk during organized competition. [AP/Wide World]

all four years, scored more than 3,000 points, and led the Trojans to two national championships, in 1983 and 1984. She injured herself in 1987 badly enough to have to retire.

Miller became an on-air commentator on men's and women's basketball for several years before being named head coach and general manager of the WNBA's Phoenix Mercury. As for not getting a chance to play in the WNBA, Miller told *Baltimore Sun* writer Kent Milton in a 1997 interview that she didn't feel sad at all. "I have no desire to play; I've had no desire to play since I walked off the floor. I think I'm one of the luckiest human beings on this planet to be able to have walked away from something knowing that I accomplished everything that I wanted to. There hasn't been a moment where I've turned around and said, 'You know, I wish I had played.' It's never been like that. I've been blessed in everything that I do. I've got a great broadcasting career and I coached a little bit at USC and now I get the opportunity to do both."

Lynette Woodard, a 6-foot guard, played her collegiate ball at the University of Kansas, where she was a four-time all-American (1978–81) and a two-time academic all-American (1980–1981). She scored an incredible 3,649 points (26.4 points per game) during

After an amazing career in college basketball, Lynette Woodard became the first female Harlem Globetrotter. [Harlem Globetrotters]

her career at Kansas, and led the nation in steals during her sophomore, junior, and senior seasons.

Woodard's success at the Olympics was followed by her becoming the first woman to play for the Harlem Globetrotters for two seasons (1985–87). It seemed inevitable that she would find her way to becoming the first woman on a team she adored. Her cousin, Hubert "Geese" Ausbie, played for the team for 24 years (1960–84) and would later become her coach. Woodard, who is a registered stockbroker, was selected by the Cleveland Rockers in the second round of the WNBA draft in 1997. At the age of 38, Woodard averaged an astounding 7.8 points per game, 4.1 rebounds per game, and 2.4 assists per game.

Woodard, who also served as the athletic director of a Kansas City, Missouri, public-school district, said that she had always felt that she'd have a chance to play professional basketball in the United States, no matter what her age. "I always said I would play, that's why I just stayed in shape because I've always played," she said to writer Kristi Nelson in an interview for the Rockers' Web site. "You may not have always known it because there wasn't always a visible stage, but yeah, I'm still playing. I'll play here, and when I leave the league, I'll still be playing."

Pat Head Summitt had proven herself to be one of the premier coaches of either gender, in any sport, with a winning percentage of .808 during 20 years at

At the 1996 Olympics, the United States defeated Brazil 111–87 for the gold medal in women's basketball. From left: Jennifer Azzi, Lisa Leslie, Carla McGhee, Katy Steding, and Sheryl Swoopes. [AP/Wide World/Susan Ragan]

the University of Tennessee. She was a standout at the University of Tennessee-Martin and played on the 1976 women's team. Summitt began coaching the Volunteers in 1974 and won national titles in 1987, 1989, and 1991. Her teams can usually be found in the Top Ten throughout the season and are contenders to win the national championship every season.

The United States took the gold in the 1988 Seoul Olympics, but would win only the bronze in 1992 in Barcelona. In 1994, the United States would see Brazil win its first World Championship, a title that the U. S.

and U.S.S.R. had dominated since the Soviet Union's inception in 1953.

The U.S. women would take the gold again at the Olympics, and once again it would be on American soil. And, just as it had been in 1984, the U. S. had assembled a Dream Team to play the world's best teams. The 1996 Atlanta Games featured a squad made up of the most talented and dedicated women to play the game: Jennifer Azzi, Ruth Bolton-Holifield, Teresa Edwards, Venus Lacey, Lisa Leslie, Rebecca Lobo, Katrina McClain, Nikki McCray, Carla McGhee, Dawn Staley, Katy Steding, and Sheryl Swoopes. Tara VanDerveer, their coach, was also a legend, with a .781 winning percentage at Idaho, Ohio, and Stanford. VanDerveer was so dedicated to winning the gold medal that she took a year off from coaching at Stanford. USA Basketball, the official organizing body for the sport in the United States, invested $3 million in the women's program.

The dedication of the team, their coach, and USA Basketball paid off. The Dream Team swept through the first seven games of the Olympics with relative ease, while racking up a record of 59–0 in less than a year, playing all comers in the way squads had barnstormed in the early part of the century. But it was in their last game, the gold medal game, that the U.S. women reestablished themselves as the world's best, as they pounded Brazil 111–87.

"The gold was won in typical fashion: strong inside play, an occasional outside shot, a big run at the start of the second half and lots of crowd-pleasing plays," wrote Chuck Schoffner of the Associated Press. "Together they trained longer and harder than any previous U.S. team. They traveled more than 100,000 miles, playing on four continents, and never lost. . . . Along the way, the U.S. team attracted a whole new legion of fans to the women's game and spurred plans for two professional leagues in this country."

The squad was led by Lisa Leslie, who scored 29 points in the final, Sheryl Swoopes, and Ruthie Bolton-Holifield. Leslie, a 6-foot 5-inch forward from USC, at first hated the game of basketball because, she says, everyone kept asking her to play. Leslie, a native of Inglewood, California, was six feet tall in the seventh grade. A friend convinced her to go out for the school's team, which she did reluctantly. By the time she was a senior in high school, she had topped a feat of Cheryl Miller's by scoring 101 points—in one half. Leslie was an all-American in 1992, 1993, and 1994 at USC, and was unanimously voted National Player of the Year in 1994. In 1993, she was voted USA Basketball's Female Athlete of the Year. She finished her collegiate career with 2,414 points (20.1 points per game), 1,214 rebounds (10.1 per game), 208 assists, and 321 blocked shots.

Sheryl Swoopes, a 6–0 guard from Texas Tech, has

equally impressive statistics. The Lubbock, Texas, native says she started playing basketball with her brothers, James and Earl, when she was seven. Little did they know their sister would set an NCAA championship game record by scoring 47 points to lead Texas Tech to an 84–82 victory over Ohio State University in the 1993 title game.

"There's always something every day you can get better at, things you can work on," Swoopes said in a 1996 interview with NBC. "Of course you're tired, and it's really hard to get out there and to keep going all the time . . . I just make myself come out every day and push myself." Swoopes averaged 24 points and 9 rebounds per game in two years (1992–4) at Texas Tech, after having spent her first two college years at a junior college. She was named Player of the Year by nine organizations in 1993, including *Sports Illustrated* and *USA Today*.

Alice "Ruthie" Bolton-Holifield was one of 20 children born to the Rev. Linwood and Leola Bolton. She excels on and off the court, having earned her degree in exercise physiology from Auburn University, and was selected to the Southeastern Conference's all-Academic team in 1988 and 1989. In 1991, Bolton-Holifield was named USA Basketball's Female Athlete of the Year and played professional basketball in Turkey and Hungary. She finished her first season with the WNBA's

Alice "Ruthie" Bolton-Holifield, one of 20 children, is not only one of the WNBA's best players, but also a first lieutenant in the U.S. Army Reserves. [AP/Wide World/Bob Galbraith]

Sacramento Monarchs averaging 19.4 points and grabbing 5.8 rebounds per game, and was a first-teamer on the all-WNBA squad.

Bolton-Holifield, who is also a first lieutenant in the U.S. Army Reserves, told WNBA.com that she had fond memories of her first season of playing professional basketball in the U.S.

"I felt good about the season, even though, obviously, we didn't make it to the playoffs," she said. "That was a disappointment, not only because we didn't make the playoffs, but we didn't really have a good season as a team. But people still loved it, they loved the intensity and the passion that we had for the sport."

If only Naismith could see where his game has gone. From peach baskets as hoops and nine guys per team in a Springfield, Massachusetts, gymnasium to Michael Jordan, tongue hanging out to the side, gliding past a defender, jumping over the outstretched arms of other players, and powering the ball into the basket with a thunderous dunk as 20,000 people explode in cheers and applause.

Basketball is now in a league with baseball and football in grabbing the attention of the American public in general and the world at large. Naismith's home country, Canada, now has two teams in the NBA—Toronto and Vancouver. Billions of dollars are spent by networks, not just showing pro basketball on television, but the college game as well. Even more money is spent by advertisers using basketball players to sell products.

The future looks bright for basketball as the world moves toward the beginning of a new century. But no matter where the game goes, it still comes down to a team of five players working together to get the ball through the hoop.

Glossary

AAU/Amateur Athletic Union: Formed in 1888, this organization is the governing body of amateur athletics in the United States.

ABL/American Basketball League: A professional basketball circuit formed in 1933 that lasted until 1953. A women's professional league, also known as the ABL, was established in 1996.

All-American: A person who is selected as the best athlete at his or her position in a particular sport.

Assist: A pass that directly leads to a basket.

Backboard: Designed in 1886, backboards, positioned around the rim and net, were used to keep spectators from interfering with the ball. Now they are used as a guide for banking the ball into the net.

BAA/Basketball Association of America: Formed in 1946, the BAA was a professional basketball circuit that lasted until 1949, when it folded into the National Basketball Association (NBA).

Block: A disruption of the flight of the ball to the net by a player.

Board: A slang term for rebound.

Bump-and-run offense: A fast-moving, physical offense where players move quickly, rotating positions in order to disrupt the defense.

Cager: Early slang term for basketball player. Refers to the wire cages that once surrounded the basketball court.

Center: A position on the basketball team; usually the tallest person, who plays in the low post, near the basket.

Center jump: Early in the game's history, the opposing centers would line up for a jump ball at the center circle after every shot.

Colored Intercollegiate Athletic Association: Formed in 1912 as the first black college athletic conference. It is now known as the Central Intercollegiate Athletic Association.

Conference: A group of schools or athletic teams that form an alliance for games, rules, etc.

Defense: Stop the opposing team from scoring. Efforts made by a player or team.

Draft/Round: Professional leagues hold drafts, where teams select nonprofessional players. Normally, each team has one pick per draft, but trades and deals can give teams more than one selection per round or, in some cases, none at all.

Dribble: What a player does in order to keep the ball bouncing and in progress. A player must dribble the ball with one hand, although he or she can switch hands. A player may not use both hands, called double-dribble, and cannot stop dribbling and start again.

Ejection: When a player or coach is thrown out of a game by a referee, usually after a fight or verbal abuse of an official.

Fast break: When the offense outruns the defense to the basket in an effort to get a shot off quickly, before the defense has time to set up.

Flagrant foul: An unnecessary and, in some cases, intentional foul; for example, grabbing or hacking a player.

Foul: An infringement of the rules of the game.

Franchise: A right or license given by a league for an owner to create a team to play in the league.

Free throw: An unhindered shot given to a player after a foul.

Guard (v.): What a player does in order to keep another from scoring, passing, or dribbling.

High post: The area around the free-throw circle.

Hook shot: A shot in which a player literally hooks the ball, either running or in a stationary position, over his shoulder toward the hoop. Kareem Abdul-Jabbar, for example, perfected the sky hook, where he would jump in the air and hook the ball over an opponent to score.

Inbound pass: When an offensive player stands out of bounds—after a foul or if the ball has gone out of play—and passes the ball to a teammate.

Jump ball: When the referee tosses the ball in the air between two players, who try to bat the ball toward a teammate.

Jump shot: When a player jumps in the air to shoot. Usually done in order to lessen the chance of a defensive player blocking the shot.

Layup: When a player, driving toward the basket uncontested, guides the ball off the backboard and into the net.

Lane (Key): The painted area between the end line and the free-throw line near each basket, outside which players line up for free throws. Also known as the key, because in the early years it was key-shaped.

Low post: The area at the base of the foul lane to either side of the basket.

Midcourt line: A line drawn from one side to the other, at the center of the court. The center circle is at the center of the midcourt line.

NAACP/The National Association for the Advancement of Colored People: Organization formed in 1909 in New York City by a group of black and white citizens committed to helping to right social injustices. It is based in Baltimore, Maryland.

NBA/National Basketball Association: Formed in 1946, the NBA is the premier league for professional basketball in the world.

NCAA/National Collegiate Athletic Association: Formed originally as the Intercollegiate Athletic Association of the United States (IAAUS) in 1906; the organization took its present name (NCAA) in 1910. It is the rule-making body for 1,200 U.S. universities and colleges, and holds championships in a host of male and female sports, except for football.

Offense: Efforts made by players in order to score.

Pass: When a player throws the ball to a teammate.

Pick: When an offensive player (standing motionless) screens a defensive player in an effort to free up a teammate to shoot or pass unhindered. The offensive player may not move with the defensive player, or an offensive penalty is called.

Pickup game: An unofficial game between players.

Quint: An early slang term used for the five players on a team.

Rebound: When a player grabs the ball after a shot fails to go in the basket.

Rookie: A first-year player.

Scrimmage: An inter-team game, normally. If against another team, the game has no inherent significance such as wins or loses during the regular season.

Shot clock: A clock that indicates the number of seconds a team has in order to shoot. In the pros, a team has 24 seconds to shoot the ball, or it is turned over. If the ball bounces off the rim, and is rebounded by the offense, the clock is reset for 24 seconds.

Showboating: Plays that display a player's or team's prowess with the ball. Dribbling between the legs and dunking were once considered showboating.

Slam dunk: When a player powers the ball through the hoop by leaping and driving the ball into the basket.

Ten-second rule: An offensive team has 10 seconds to move the ball out of their defensive end after inbounding the ball. If they cannot, the opposing team gets the ball.

Three-point line: A visible arc around the perimeter of the key, which divides two-point plays inside the arc, and three-point shots outside the arc.

Three-second lane violation: A penalty is called if a player stands in the key for more than three seconds.

WNBA/Women's National Basketball Association: A women's pro league—sponsored by the NBA—which began in 1997.

Bibliography

Bibliography

Ashe, Arthur. *A Hard Road to Glory: The History of the African-American Athlete 1619–1919.* New York: Warner Books, 1988.

Ashe, Arthur. *A Hard Road to Glory: The History of the African-American Athlete 1919–1945.* New York: Warner Books, 1988.

Chalk, Ocania. *Black College Sport.* New York: Dodd, Mead & Co., 1976.

Franklin, John Hope, and Alfred A. Moss, Jr. *From Slavery to Freedom: A History of Negro Americans.* New York: Alfred A. Knopf, 1994.

George, Nelson. *Elevating the Game: Black Men and Basketball.* New York: HarperCollins, 1992.

Haskins, James. *From Lew Alcindor to Kareem Abdul-Jabbar.* New York: Lothrop, Lee and Shepard Co., 1972.

McKissack, Fredrick L., Jr., and Patricia C. McKissack. *Black Diamond: The Story of the Negro Baseball Leagues.* New York: Scholastic Inc., 1994.

Peterson, Robert W. *Cages to Jump Shots: Pro Basketball's Early Years*. New York: Oxford University Press, 1990.

Rader, Benjamin G. *American Sports*. Englewood, New Jersey: Prentice-Hall, Inc., 1985.

Ruft, David, and Richard M. Cohen. *The Sports Encyclopedia: Pro Basketball*. New York: St. Martin's Press, 1988.

Rust, Art, Jr., and Edna Rust. *Art Rust's Illustrated History of the Black Athlete*. New York: Doubleday and Co., 1985.

Sachare, Alex. *100 Greatest Basketball Players of All Time*. New York: Pocket Books, 1997.

Sherrow, Victoria. *Encyclopedia of Women and Sports*. Santa Barbara, California: ABC-Clio, 1996.

Young, A. J. "Doc." *Negro Firsts in Sports*. Chicago: Johnson Publications, 1963.

INTERNET RESOURCES

Full Court Press: The Women's Basketball Journal (www.fullcourt.com)

The History of Women's Basketball (httpsrv.ocs.drexel.edu/admin/vaughnmv)

www.wnba.com
www.msnbc.com

Index